THE IMPORTANCE OF

Charlemagne

These and other titles are included in The Importance Of biography series:

Alexander the Great	Harry Houdini
Muhammad Ali	Thomas Jefferson
Louis Armstrong	Mother Jones
James Baldwin	Chief Joseph
Clara Barton	Joe Louis
Charlemagne	Malcolm X
Napoleon Bonaparte	Thurgood Marshall
Julius Caesar	Margaret Mead
Rachel Carson	Michelangelo
Charlie Chaplin	Wolfgang Amadeus Mozart
Cesar Chavez	John Muir
Winston Churchill	Sir Isaac Newton
Cleopatra	Richard M. Nixon
Christopher Columbus	Georgia O'Keeffe
Hernando Cortes	Louis Pasteur
Marie Curie	Pablo Picasso
Amelia Earhart	Elvis Presley
Thomas Edison	Jackie Robinson
Albert Einstein	Norman Rockwell
Duke Ellington	Anwar Sadat
Dian Fossey	Margaret Sanger
Benjamin Franklin	Oskar Schindler
Galileo Galilei	John Steinbeck
Emma Goldman	Tecumseh
Jane Goodall	Jim Thorpe
Martha Graham	Mark Twain
Stephen Hawking	Queen Victoria
Jim Henson	Pancho Villa
Adolf Hitler	H. G. Wells

THE IMPORTANCE OF

Charlemagne

by
Timothy Levi Biel

Lucent Books, P.O. Box 289011, San Diego, CA 92198-9011

Library of Congress Cataloging-in-Publication Data

Biel, Timothy L.
    The importance of Charlemagne / by Timothy Levi Biel.
       p.   cm.—(The importance of)
    Includes bibliographical references and index.
    Summary: A biography of the Frankish warrior and king
who built a great empire in western Europe.
    ISBN 1-56006-074-3 (alk. paper)
    1. Charlemagne, Emperor, 742–814—Juvenile literature.
2. Holy Roman Empire—Kings and rulers—Biography—
Juvenile literature.   3. France—History—To 987—Juvenile
literature.   4. Civilization, Medieval—Juvenile literature.
[1. Charlemagne, Emperor, 742–814.   2. Kings, queens,
rulers, etc.   3. France—History—To 987.]   I. Title. II. Series.
    DC73.B44   1997
    944'.014'092—dc21   96–45625
                                    CIP
                                     AC

Contents

Foreword

THE IMPORTANCE OF biography series deals with individuals who have made a unique contribution to history. The editors of the series have deliberately chosen to cast a wide net and include people from all fields of endeavor. Individuals from politics, music, art, literature, philosophy, science, sports, and religion are all represented. In addition, the editors did not restrict the series to individuals whose accomplishments have helped change the course of history. Of necessity, this criterion would have eliminated many whose contribution was great, though limited. Charles Darwin, for example, was responsible for radically altering the scientific view of the natural history of the world. His achievements continue to impact the study of science today. Others, such as Chief Joseph of the Nez Percé, played a pivotal role in the history of their own people. While Joseph's influence does not extend much beyond the Nez Percé, his nonviolent resistance to white expansion and his continuing role in protecting his tribe and his homeland remain an inspiration to all.

These biographies are more than factual chronicles. Each volume attempts to emphasize an individual's contributions both in his or her own time and for posterity. For example, the voyages of Christopher Columbus opened the way to European colonization of the New World. Unquestionably, his encounter with the New World brought monumental changes to both Europe and the Americas in his day. Today, however, the broader impact of Columbus's voyages is being critically scrutinized. *Christopher Columbus,* as well as every biography in The Importance Of series, includes and evaluates the most recent scholarship available on each subject.

Each author includes a wide variety of primary and secondary source quotations to document and substantiate his or her work. All quotes are footnoted to show readers exactly how and where biographers derive their information, as well as provide stepping stones to further research. These quotations enliven the text by giving readers eyewitness views of the life and times of each individual covered in The Importance Of series.

Finally, each volume is enhanced by photographs, bibliographies, chronologies, and comprehensive indexes. For both the casual reader and the student engaged in research, The Importance Of biographies will be a fascinating adventure into the lives of people who have helped shape humanity's past and present, and who will continue to shape its future.

IMPORTANT DATES IN THE LIFE OF CHARLEMAGNE

742
Birth of Charles the Great.

760–768
Pepin III and his son Charles the Great lead expeditions to Aquitaine.

768
Death of Pepin III. Frankish kingdom divided between Charles and Carloman.

769
Charles leads victorious campaign in Aquitaine.

770
Charles disowns Himiltrude and marries Desiderata, daughter of the Lombard king.

771
Charles disowns Desiderata, marries Hildegard, breaks with Carloman. Death of Carloman.

773
Charles invades Lombardia and lays siege to Pavia.

774
Charles makes his first visit to Rome. Pavia falls and Charles declares himself king of Lombardia as well as Frankia.

775
Charles invades Saxony, defeating both the Westphalians and Eastphalians.

777
General Assembly at Paderborn to declare the annexation of Saxony.

778
Charles's unsuccessful invasion of Spain. Defeat at Roncesvaux (the origin of the legend of Roland). Birth of Louis the Pious. Witikind leads Saxon raids on Austrasian border.

781
Charles's second visit to Rome. Hadrian baptizes Pepin (born Carloman) and Louis anoints them as kings of Italy and Aquitaine, respectively.

782
Charles's mass execution of forty-five hundred Saxons at Verden.

783
Death of Queen Hildegard. Death of Bertrada, Charles's mother. Charles marries Fastrada.

784
Charles's devastation of Saxony. Tens of thousands of Saxons die from flooding and famine. Charles keeps the Frankish army in Saxony throughout the winter.

785
Witikind surrenders.

787
Charles's third visit to Rome. Invasion of Bavaria and submission of Tassilo, duke of Bavaria.

788
Tassilo found guilty of treason and stripped of his title as duke of Bavaria. Bavaria is annexed.

793
Failure of Karlsgraben, Charles's canal project.

794
Death of Queen Fastrada. Charles marries Liutgarda.

795
Franks under King Pepin conquer and plunder the Ring of the Avars in Hungary. Death of Pope Hadrian III. Leo III elected pope.

797
Charles conquers Wihmodia and deports fifty thousand Saxons.

799
Conspiracy in Rome leaves Pope Leo III near death. Pope Leo escapes imprisonment. Charles receives him in Paderborn.

800
Death of Queen Liutgarda at Tours. Reception of Charles at Rome. Trial of Pope Leo III. Charles crowned emperor by Leo III.

801
Louis the Pious captures Barcelona and other Spanish strongholds, establishing the Spanish March.

806
Charles announces plan for partitioning the empire among his three sons.

810
Death of King Pepin, son of Charles the Great.

811
Death of Charles, son of Charles the Great.

813
Charles's great Rhine bridge at Mainz goes up in flames. Charles becomes ill, sends for Louis, his son. Louis the Pious acclaimed and crowned as associate emperor.

814
Death of Charles the Great. Buried in the Basilica of St. Mary at Aix-la-Chapelle. Louis becomes emperor.

840
Death of Louis the Pious.

841
Battle of Fontenoy.

843
Treaty of Verdun permanently breaks up the Holy Roman Empire.

A Founder of Nations

Few names in European history inspire greater thoughts of medieval romance and glory than Charlemagne. In fact, only mythical figures like King Arthur, Sir Lancelot, Robin Hood, and Charlemagne's own loyal servant Roland have inspired as many legends as Charlemagne, who lived from 742 to 814. One reason for Charlemagne's prominence in medieval lore was his historic role in establishing the traditions of European royalty and nobility.

Another reason for Charlemagne's prominence was his interest in education and the arts. He invited scholars and artists throughout Europe and England to work and live at his court, and he financed the finest library collections in the Western world. As a result, more written history has been preserved about this early medieval king than about many later rulers. About A.D. 830, Einhard, Charles's close friend, adviser, and administrator in his royal government, wrote a biography entitled *Vita Caroli* (*The Life of Charlemagne*), which has been preserved to this day. Capitularies, or collections of official decrees, provide written records of Charles's reign, as do annals, or unofficial records, which have also survived.

These records capture a critical time in Western history, the formative period known as the Early Middle Ages. Although the Holy Roman Empire that Charle-magne founded began to crumble just twenty-seven years after his death, his influence lived on in the military and cultural traditions of the European nobility; in the secular power of the Roman Catholic Church; and in the restoration of art, literature, and education, which he began. Thanks to Charles's conquests, his contemporary noblemen thought of themselves not so much as French, German, or Italian, but rather as Europeans, loyal subjects of a single monarch. They shared a common culture, a common religious liturgy and tradition, a common education, and even a common court language—Latin.

A Legendary Figure

The legends of Charlemagne's deeds soon outgrew reality. In addition to his actual conquests, the legendary Charlemagne was credited with conquests in Aquitaine, Italy, and Burgundy that had really been achieved by his father and his grandfather. According to legend, Charlemagne saved Europe from being overrun by the Muslim caliphs who ruled in Spain. In reality, geographical and political factors made the Muslims of Spain an unlikely threat to northern Europe.

Charlemagne, depicted here at his coronation, is credited with establishing the traditions that shaped European royalty for centuries. His reign also started a revival of art, literature, and education.

So far as we know, no one referred to this important king as "Charlemagne" until after his death. In fact, the inscription on his tombstone reads "Here lies Charles the Great," and no historian would argue against his claim to greatness.

Because the legend has grown so much bigger than the historical figure, historians today use the name Charlemagne cautiously, knowing that it may imply the legendary figure rather than the historical one. By whatever name he is called, Charles the Great, king of the Franks and founder of the Holy Roman Empire, left an indelible mark on the map, the culture, and the governments of Europe.

1 The Rise of the Franks

Charles the Great's conquests and advancement of civilization over so much of Europe is often considered a kind of miracle. A glance back at his heritage, though, shows that Charles's empire did not spring miraculously to life. Indeed, many of the customs of his kingdom and its relative civility grew out of the marriage of Frankish and Roman cultures. What Charles accomplished, above all, was to complete building his empire on the foundations laid by earlier Frankish rulers.

The Great Migration

Until the fall of Rome in A.D. 476, much of what is now France, bordered by the Rhine River and the Alps in the east and by the Atlantic Ocean and the Pyrenees Mountains in the west, was a Roman colony. The Romans called this region Gaul, and they referred to the primitive natives of Gaul as the Gallic people.

East of Gaul and beyond the Alps lay the vast unconquered lands that the Romans called Germania. In the fourth century A.D., warlike tribes from Germania migrated in huge numbers to Gaul, beginning what historians call the Great Migration.

The Franks and the Alamans from western Germania came to settle in northeastern France, roughly between the Rhine and the Seine Rivers. Members of the Angle and Saxon tribes, also from western Germania, migrated throughout what is now Denmark, the Netherlands, and England. The Angles and Saxons forced many of the native English Celts and Britons across the English Channel

The Gauls (pictured) were natives of an area that is roughly equal to present-day France. Gaul was occupied first by the Romans, and then by migrating tribes from Germania in the fourth century.

The first invasion of the Franks into Gaul, shown here, was part of the Great Migration of tribes from the east settling in western Europe. The Franks occupied northeastern France, and they were left relatively alone as others fought over the remnants of the Roman Empire.

into northwestern France, which became known as Brittany. From eastern Germania, the Visigoths migrated toward western Gaul, dominating the regions we now call Bordeaux and Provence. The Burgundians also came from eastern Germania and settled the eastern part of Gaul, which became known as Burgundy. One last Germanic tribe, also from the east, was the Lombards, who dominated much of Italy, including Rome, which the Lombards sacked, or destroyed, in 476.

With the fall of Rome came a great splintering of power in Europe. For the next three centuries, Italy, which had been the heart of culture, religion, and political authority for all of Europe, became a battleground for a long and bitter struggle between the Lombards and the Byzantines. The Byzantine Empire, founded by the emperor Constantine in 330 as the eastern part of the Roman Empire, dominated Asia Minor and the eastern Mediter-

ranean region for better than eight centuries. The Byzantines even ruled most of Italy for a short time, until they were defeated by the Lombards in 568.

This dramatic power struggle in southern Europe and the Mediterranean left the tribes of Gaul and northern Europe to develop on their own. Even though the Roman Empire had been dismantled in the West, some descendants of Roman military commanders and governors held onto their lands in Gaul and served the Germanic warriors. Procopius, a fifth-century Greek historian, explains how these Romans joined the Germanic armies without giving up many of their traditional Roman customs:

Now other Roman soldiers had been stationed at the frontiers of Gaul to serve as guards. . . . They gave themselves, together with their military standards and the land which they had long been guarding for the Romans, to the . . . Germans; and they handed down to their offspring all the customs of their fathers, which were thus preserved, and this people has held them in sufficient reverence to guard them even up to my time. For even at the present day they are clearly recognized as belonging to the legions to which they were assigned when they served in ancient times, and they always carry their own standards when they enter battle, and always follow the customs of their fathers. And they preserve the dress of the Romans in every particular, even as regards their shoes.[1]

Roman traditions, then, did not die out altogether after the fall of the Roman government. In fact, the Roman Church exerted a strong influence on European life. Monasteries were scattered throughout much of Gaul, and even throughout England. These outposts of Christianity in a predominantly pagan land gradually began to influence the leaders of various Germanic tribes, especially the so-called Merovingian kings, who were descendants of the Frankish warlord Meroveus.

Clovis: The First of the Merovingian Kings and Founder of the Frankish Nobility

The first and most powerful of the Merovingian kings was Clovis, who conquered many of the tribal chieftains throughout Gaul and declared himself *rex*, or king, of Frankia, the land of the Frankish people. Clovis's conquests extended his kingdom from the Alps to the Pyrenees, where he is believed to have ruled as king from about 481 until 511. In 496 he personally adopted Christianity and commanded that all of his subjects do the same.

From church leaders and Roman descendants, Clovis learned about the Roman legal system and government hierarchy. He admired the hierarchy of the Roman Church and blended the concept with traditional Frankish customs. As a result, Clovis built the first aristocratic Frankish government, which became the dominant model for most European governments until the twentieth century. He divided Gaul into about one hundred counties. Many of these counties, such as Troyes, Flanders, Anjou, Blois, Provence, Champagne, and Burgundy, still exist with

Clovis conquered the local chieftains in Gaul and became the first king of Frankia in about 481. His government was a blend of Roman and Frankish traditions.

the same names they were given during Clovis's reign. His most loyal generals, who became known as *comtes* (in English, counts) ruled the counties.

Frankish Kings and the Roman Church Form a Powerful Alliance

To get Clovis's approval, his subjects began to adopt his religion, so churches and shrines to the saints started to appear throughout the Frankish realm after 496. The display of religion at a time when most Germanic peoples still worshiped their pagan gods made Clovis very popular with the Roman Church leaders. The church sent a bishop to each Frankish county to oversee the building of churches and the spread of Christianity. The presence of both counts and bishops led to occasional rivalry and competition, but it also built a strong alliance that fostered the growth of two elite institutions: the Frankish nobility, or class of landholders, and the church.

Barbaric Franks: A Foreigner's View

By the time Clovis became their king in 481, the Franks had already gained fame for their bravery and their ruthlessness. The fifth-century Greek historian Procopius describes these qualities in his Gothic Wars, *translated and edited by H. B. Dewing.*

"Forgetting for the moment their oaths and the treaties they had made a little before with the Romans and the Goths (for this nation in matters of trust is the most treacherous in the world), they straightway gathered to the number of one hundred thousand under the leadership of Theudebert, and marched into Italy. They had a small body of cavalry about their leader, and these were the only ones armed with spears, while all the rest were foot-soldiers having neither bows nor spears, but each man carried a sword and shield and one axe. Now the iron head of this weapon was thick and exceedingly sharp on both sides, while the wooden handle was very short. And they were accustomed always to throw these axes at one signal in the first charge, and thus to shatter the shields of the enemy and kill the men.

These barbarians, though they have become Christians, preserve the greater part of their ancient religion; for they still make human sacrifices and other sacrifices of an unholy nature, and it is in connection with these that they make their prophecies."

Clovis, shown here in battle, divided Frankia into counties and appointed a count to rule each one. As the later Merovingian kings weakened, the local counts gained power.

Clovis had been a powerful and influential ruler, but the idea of a central government led by a king was not part of Frankish culture. These people's daily activities centered around protecting their lands and crops from natural disasters and hostile neighbors. They needed a king only when they felt threatened by a powerful foreign enemy.

Thus, when Clovis died in 511, his kingdom was divided among his four sons. Throughout most of the sixth and seventh centuries, three Frankish kingdoms—Austrasia, Neustria, and Burgundy—were ruled by descendants of Clovis. The generations of relatively weak leaders are collectively known as the Merovingian kings. Occasionally, through inheritance, marriage, or war, one king might rule two or even all three of these kingdoms, but for the most part, the real power of government lay in the hands of the local counts and bishops.

The Frankish Village Remains Isolated and Independent

From the middle of the sixth century until the time of Charlemagne, the rural village remained the central unit of Frankish culture. Each village was ruled by a village lord and dominated by a village church or monastery. Most villages were surrounded by great forests and meadows that teemed with plants and wildlife. The peasants, who made up 90 percent of the population, awoke every morning to the clamor of huge flocks of birds. Herds of deer browsed in the fields and clearings around the village. Wild boars often ravaged the grain fields, as did rabbits and foxes, and wolves constantly took advantage of the poultry and oxen.

Like the wild wolves, the small class of noblemen who owned the land claimed the meadows and forests and all the natural riches that filled them. Although their homes and furnishings were crude when compared to those of their counterparts in the more advanced Byzantine and Muslim civilizations to the east, members of the noble class (including the bishops

The Baptism of Clovis

"Before [Clovis] could say a word, all those present shouted in unison: We will give up worshipping our mortal gods, pious king, and we are prepared to follow the immortal God about whom Remigious [Bishop of Rheims] preaches. . . . The public squares were draped with colored [or painted] cloths, the churches were adorned with white hangings, the baptistry was prepared, sticks of incense gave off clouds of perfume, sweet-smelling candles gleamed bright and the holy place of baptism was filled with divine fragrance. . . . Like some new Constantine, he stepped forward to the baptismal pool . . . and the holy man of God addressed him in these pregnant words: Bow your head in meekness, Sicamber. Worship what you have burnt, burn what you have been wont to worship."

Clovis's conversion to Christianity and baptism (pictured) marked the beginning of Christianity as a growing trend among the Franks, who previously worshiped pagan gods.

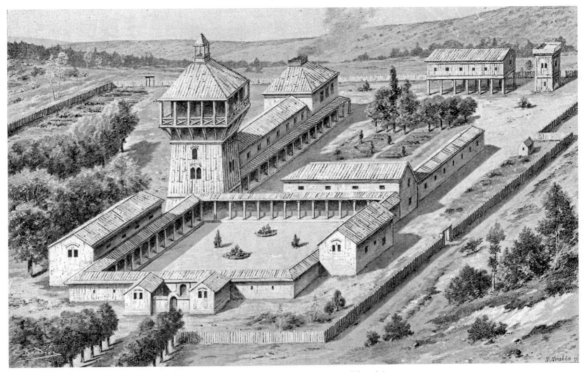

Each Frankish village was ruled by a lord, who lived on an estate like this one. While the nobility had comfortable houses, the peasants of the village lived in huts made from sticks and mud.

and abbots who ran the churches and monasteries) lived in relative comfort.

While the families of nobility lived in stone houses and wrapped themselves in furs and fine leathers, most villagers wore one rough linen dress, shirt, or pair of britches until it wore out. In the winter, they wore wool cloaks and caps and rough leather shoes without hard soles. In their sticks-and-mud huts, entire families shared one or two blankets as their only protection from the cold. Even building a fire was a luxury, for although there was plenty of firewood in the surrounding forests, it belonged to the noble lord who owned the land. The fish in the streams, the deer in the fields, and the birds in the trees were all off-limits to the peasants, many of whom died from starvation or illness every winter.

The death of a few peasants was of no greater concern to the typical nobleman than the loss of a few cattle. Prior to the twelfth century, peasant labor was abundant and cheap. No self-respecting nobleman of the seventh century did his own manual labor. The backbreaking jobs were left to the peasants.

Most Frankish noblemen spent little time in their own villages. Instead, they held court in their castles or attended court in the castle of a superior lord. When they gathered at court, they judged complaints of one lord unfairly

A king receives his vassal. When a king granted land to a noble, the noble became the king's vassal and swore a feudal oath to defend the king whenever called upon.

taking another's property, or conflicting claims to land, based on obscure and complicated inheritance customs. These rich men enjoyed great feasts and entertainment and frequently hunted together or held tournaments, that is, contests that tested their battle skills.

Noblemen as Private Soldiers: The Origins of Feudalism

When not meeting with their fellow noblemen at court, they often met each other on the battlefield. Private warfare among nobles was an inevitable by-product of feudalism, the system of private government and military service that began during the time of the weak Merovingian kings. The word *feudalism* comes from *feudum*, the Latin word for fief, which means a piece of land granted by one nobleman to another. When one nobleman received a fief from another, the recipient swore a feudal oath making himself a vassal, or loyal servant, to the donor. The vassal referred to the other nobleman as his liege or his lord. A county, for example, was a fief granted to a count by his king. In return, the count swore a feudal oath to defend the king's interests and to fight for him whenever called upon. Just as counts swore feudal oaths to their kings, viscounts received fiefs from counts by swearing feudal oaths to them, and village lords obtained their land and noble status by swearing oaths to the village lords above them.

The result was a network of political alliances that enabled a great lord to call his vassals either to court or to war. If called to war, a vassal was expected to call upon his vassals, who would in turn call upon their own vassals. Initially, the fiefs, the titles of nobility, and the feudal obligations that went with them endured only a single lifetime. As a practical matter, however, when a nobleman died, his sons most often assumed his feudal obligations, and usually the oldest son assumed the noble title. By the seventh century, this practice had become so common that feudal oaths and titles were normally considered hereditary.

Arnulf and Pepin I: Charlemagne's Noble Ancestry

Despite frequent private wars, the feudal system helped bring much of Gaul under the rule of the Merovingian kings and their vassals. In 613 the Merovingian king Clothar II awarded new titles to two powerful and wealthy Frankish families in Austrasia for their strong military and diplomatic support. The head of one of these families, Arnulf, was named Bishop of Metz, the richest and most important city in the realm. Pepin, the head of the other loyal family, was named mayor of the palace of Austrasia. With this noble title came the responsibility of looking after all of the king's lands, or royal domains. Pepin acquired even more power when Clothar divided his kingdom and made his ten-year-old son, Dagobert, king of Austrasia. As Dagobert's chief counselor, Pepin ruled Austrasia in all but name until Dagobert came of age. Through the middle of the seventh century, Pepin and Arnulf remained among the most powerful noblemen in Frankia, but historians remember them for being the great-great-

---

The Inglorious Merovingian Kings

Gregory of Tours's History of the Franks *contains this scathing rebuke of the Merovingian kings.*

"The Franks ought, indeed, to have been warned by the sad fate of earlier kings, who, through their inability ever to agree with one another, were killed by their enemies. . . . Just think of all Clovis achieved, Clovis, the founder of your victorious country, who slaughtered those rulers who opposed him, conquered hostile peoples and captured their territories, thus bequeathing to you absolute and unquestioned dominion over them! At the time when he accomplished all this, he possessed neither gold nor silver such as you have in your treasure houses! But you, what are you doing? . . . you cannot keep peace, and therefore you do not know the grace of God."

great-grandfathers of Charlemagne. They are the earliest known roots to one of the greatest European dynasties of all time: the Carolingian dynasty. When Arnulf's son Ansegisel married Pepin's daughter Begga, these two roots merged to form the trunk of Charlemagne's family tree. Over the next century, Charlemagne's ancestors ruled as mayors of the palace of Austrasia and helped make it the most powerful in the Frankish kingdoms.

The Influence of Pepin II as Mayor of the Palace

In 687, Pepin II, the grandson of both Arnulf and Pepin I, helped the Merovingian king Theuderic III gain control of all three Frankish realms—Neustria, Austrasia, and Burgundy. Over the next thirty years, Pepin II built a strong feudal network among the loyal nobility in his Austrasian homeland. The *Annals of Metz*, a history written in the eighth century, describes the important annual general assemblies of Frankish noblemen, and it leaves little doubt about who was in charge of these assemblies:

> Each year at the beginning of March, the mayor of the palace, Pepin II, convened a general assembly with all the Franks according to ancient custom. On account of the reverence due to the royal title, he had the king preside until he had received the yearly gifts offered by all the leading men among the Franks; made a plea for peace and for the protection of the churches of God, and of orphans and widows; forbidden the raping of women and the crime of arson; and ordered the army

to be ready for departure on the appointed day. Then Pepin sent the king away to his royal villa at Montmacq to be guarded with honor and veneration, while Pepin himself governed the Frankish kingdom.[2]

Pepin II also extended Frankish influence in Gaul. He appointed bishops and directed them to build monasteries in Aquitaine, in what is now central and southern France. Continuing the strong alliance with the Roman Church, he recognized the growing wealth and political power of the bishoprics and abbeys and the families that controlled them. He es-

Pepin I was named mayor of the palace of Austrasia by the Frankish king in 613. Pepin's powerful position set the stage for his descendants, including Charlemagne, who would make up the Carolingian dynasty.

tablished new monasteries and abbeys throughout Austrasia and increased the landholdings of others. A document signed by Pepin II and his wife Plectrude, dated May 13, 706, certifies the granting of land to an Abbot Willibrord. It also shows how Pepin used such grants to secure the loyalty of their holders:

> When Willibrord passes from this life, his brothers will freely choose an abbot. This man should show himself faithful in all things to us, to our son Grimoald, to his son, and to the sons of Drogo, our grandsons.[3]

This bond between the church and the Frankish nobility influenced European history for centuries to come.

As Pepin approached the end of his long life, having outlived his own sons, he had to decide who would inherit his position as mayor of the palace and duke of Austrasia. Ultimately he chose an illegitimate grandson, Theodoald. Thus, when Pepin II died on December 16, 714, his six-year-old grandson became mayor of the palace and duke of Austrasia.

Without Pepin II's strong personality to hold them together, his fragile political alliances broke apart. The Neustrians, who had grudgingly accepted their feudal obligations to the Austrasian Pepinids, seized Pepin's death as an opportunity to defy their feudal oaths. They established their own mayor of the palace of Neustria, and he quickly removed Pepin II's former followers from positions of power in their kingdom. The once-powerful house of Pepin had lost many of its vassals and much of its land and wealth.

Chapter

2 Founders of the Carolingian Dynasty

The house of Pepin might have faded into history after the death of Pepin II had it not been for his bastard son, Charles Martel. Charles Martel, the grandfather of Charlemagne, was the first in his family line to bear the name Charles. From his name comes the term *Carolingian*, or "descendant of Charles," which historians have used to label the dynasty of Frankish kings that followed the Merovingians. The name Martel, which means "the hammer" in Latin, was added by later Carolingian historians to signify Charles's military and political strength. Like his father, Pepin II, Charles Martel never held the title of king. Also like his father, he employed political and military savvy to establish himself as the virtual ruler of the three Frankish realms.

Charles earned his position in spite of having his stepmother, Plectrude, as his archenemy. Plectrude held the real decision-making power for her grandson Theodoald, whom Charles wanted to overthrow. Plectrude suspected as much, so she had Charles Martel arrested and held prisoner at their palace in Metz.

However, most of Pepin II's former vassals favored Charles over Theodoald, and in 716 they helped Charles escape. A year later, with Charles leading them, the vassals assembled an army and drove the Neustrians out of Austrasia, back across the Meuse River. They promptly proclaimed Charles the new Austrasian mayor of the palace and named a Merovingian prince, Clothar IV, the new Austrasian king.

But Charles was not content to stop there. He wanted to reclaim the control that his father had held over Neustria,

Charles Martel, Charlemagne's grandfather, never held the title of king, but nonetheless he aspired to control all three Frankish realms—Neustria, Austrasia, and Burgundy.

Charles Martel displays his military prowess. With Austrasia already under his rule, Charles marched on Paris and seized power in Neustria, as well as Burgundy and the surrounding duchies.

Burgundy, and the surrounding duchies. Therefore, Charles marched on Paris, the capital city of Neustria, and quickly seized power.

One way of cementing his control in these regions was to reclaim lands that his ancestors had once given to the church and place his own vassals in charge of them. Citing the need to defend the church from outside enemies, Charles assigned church land as fiefs to noblemen who swore loyalty to him. In other cases, he appointed his vassals as bishops and ab-bots. As a result, many men who became bishops and abbots throughout the Frankish realms had no religious training but plenty of military experience.

Though these practices damaged the church's respectability, they were politically effective. In fact, Charles Martel is sometimes unfairly remembered by historians more for secularizing church lands than for his many other accomplishments. In reality, he merely carried on a practice that had begun long before his time and would continue for centuries afterward.

Corruption in the Frankish Church

Under Charles Martel, the church became a tool of political expansion. In 740, Archbishop Boniface, who had helped spread Christianity throughout the Frankish kingdom, wrote a letter to the pope complaining about this corruption. The letter is quoted by Pierre Riché in The Carolingians.

"The Franks have not convened a synod in more than 80 years; they have no archbishops; they have nowhere established or restored the statutory rules governing episcopal sees [church districts supervised by bishops]; and in most cases, the bishoprics have been handed over to greedy laymen, or to adulterous, undedicated clerical carousers who profit from them in a worldly way. . . .

They do battle with the army, and bearing weapons they shed human blood with their own hands, of both pagans and Christians.

As for the so-called deacons, they wallow from their adolescence in debauchery and adultery, with four, five, or more concubines in their bed each night, and they do not blush to read the Gospel and move on to the priestly order, and then to the episcopacy."

Archbishop Boniface was disgusted by the church officials whom Charles Martel appointed, claiming they were adulterous, greedy, and fought in battle.

Even though he took over some lands from the church in Frankia, he lent military and financial support to establishing several new churches and monasteries in the German regions of Saxony, Bavaria, and Alemannia. Charles offered a peaceful alliance to the powerful noble families in these regions if they granted some of their land to the church. Then he installed his followers and relatives as abbots and bishops. In this way, he helped expand Frankish influence into eastern Germany.

During his reign, Charles not only reunited Austrasia, Neustria, and Burgundy but also conquered Aquitaine and the independent kingdom of Provence. He expanded the Frankish kingdom to a size somewhat larger than modern France, reaching from the English Channel in the north to the Mediterranean in the south and from the Atlantic coast to the Rhine River. Over the entire kingdom, Charles ruled as king, except in name. In fact, when the Merovingian king Theuderic died in 737, Charles did not bother naming a successor. A letter from Pope Gregory III, written in 739, even addresses Charles as *vice regulus*, or "substitute king." [4]

The Death of Charles Martel Leads to Anarchy

On October 22, 741, at the relatively old age of sixty, after ruling the Frankish kingdom for a quarter of a century, Charles Martel died. Although Charles had never assumed the title of king, most Franks apparently thought of him as their king. The official entry in the daily records for the Echternach Abbey, for instance, identifies that day in 741 with the death of King Charles. The most telling sign of Charles Martel's importance to the stability of the Frankish kingdom, however, was the state of anarchy that swept through the land after his death.

A few months earlier, knowing that he was dying, Charles divided most of his kingdom between two sons, Carloman, the oldest, and Pepin III, also known as Pepin the Short, the father of Charlemagne. Predictably, many Frankish noblemen viewed Charles Martel's death as an opportunity to advance their own positions. Once more, the entire kingdom was beset by open revolt.

Childeric III, the Last of the Puppet Kings

Realizing that their power remained insecure, Carloman and Pepin III selected a young man from the monastery of St. Bertin, whom they believed to be a Merovingian, and set him up as king with the name Childeric III. It may seem illogical to modern political sense that this Merovingian king, who was nothing more than a puppet of Carloman and Pepin, could have commanded any respect from his subjects. Yet to many Franks, the image of a king who claimed that he could trace his ancestors back to mythical times was important. The Merovingian king represented the single person to whom all his subjects owed their allegiance.

Carloman and Pepin recognized that their father's failure to name a king after Theuderic died had given many dukes in the conquered territories an excuse to rebel. The new king, Childeric, content to allow the mayors to rule his kingdom for

Childeric III, a Merovingian, ruled in name only. Charles Martel's sons, who held the true power, recognized that a king with an established name was integral to uniting the Frankish people.

him, declared in an official charter that he was "happy to have been reestablished on the throne."[5] The Frankish people also seemed content to have Childeric as their king, making it easier for Carloman and Pepin III to rule in peace and harmony.

Carloman and Boniface Reform the Frankish Church

Once relative peace had been restored, the two palace mayors realized that the Franks' conversion to Christianity over the past century had been incomplete. Many who had become priests or monks had done so to gain wealth and political favor. Even bishops and abbots were often illiterate or poorly trained in Scripture and Christian doctrine. At the same time, many of the common people still prac-

ticed animal sacrifices, magical curses and incantations, prophecies, and other pagan rituals or mixed their traditional pagan religion with Christian rituals and beliefs.

Carloman was more concerned with these conditions than was his brother, Pepin III. Carloman had become a close friend of Archbishop Boniface, the famous English monk who had helped lead the Christianizing of Germanic tribes under Charles Martel. Together, Boniface and Carloman convinced Pepin III that if the church did not remain strong and stable, then neither would their kingdom. Therefore, Boniface was asked to convene a synod, or church council of all the bishops in the kingdom, to reform the church and reinforce the people's faith in it.

This so-called Germanic Council opened in Metz on April 21, 742. Written records of that council reveal that Carloman presided over the meetings and addressed the thousands of bishops, abbots, monks, priests, and nuns in attendance:

> On the advice of servants of God and of his leading followers, Carloman convened the bishops and priests of his realm to consult them about restoring the laws of God and of the church corrupted in the time of previous leaders, so that Christian people might ensure thereby the salvation of their souls and not be led astray by false ministers.[6]

As a result of the reforms passed by the Germanic Council, married priests were asked to give up either their families or the priesthood. Monks and priests who kept mistresses were forced to leave the ministry, and those who were considered extremely decadent were locked in dungeons. All ordained monks and priests, including bishops and abbots, were required to wear robes that distinguished them from the laity. They were also forbidden to shed the blood of others, even in battle. Although this order was broken frequently during the Middle Ages, it has remained an official policy of the church to this day.

Frankish Nobility Takes Advantage of Church Wealth

These reforms may have helped protect the church from some corruption, at least for a brief period, but as long as the institution remained influential, powerful, and wealthy, it continued to attract noble families who were more interested in serving themselves than others. This was especially true in the highest positions, which controlled the greatest wealth and power.

From Rome, Pope Zacharias tried to regain control of the Carolingian bishops and abbots by assigning his own archbishops to oversee them and name their successors, but this plan met such strong opposition that it was soon abandoned. One of those most vigorously opposed to the pope's involvement was Pepin III, who viewed it as a foreign intrusion.

Carloman, who shared power with Pepin III, disagreed with his brother on this issue of investiture, or the appointing of church officials. He and Boniface agreed with the church, which viewed itself as a higher authority than either the king or the palace mayors. Carloman even gave several of his own domains in Austrasia to the church for the establishment of new abbeys, and he granted the pope the right to name the abbots. One of these, the abbey of Fulda, was granted to Boniface as a reward for his many years of faithful service.

Carloman found himself disagreeing with his brother more and more. After Boniface, his closest friend and adviser, retired to Fulda, Carloman grew weary of political battles and wars and became increasingly interested in the church. In

---

The Do-Nothing Kings

Einhard, Charles's adviser and biographer, labeled the Merovingian kings the do-nothing kings and described the limited powers of King Childeric III in The Life of Charlemagne.

"Childeric III had only the satisfaction of sitting on his throne with his long hair and his flowing beard. He had to be content to hold audiences for ambassadors from various lands and possessed a single, poor domain with a house and a few servants. When he had to travel, he got into an ox-drawn cart led by a drover in the rustic manner. In this turn-out, he journeyed to the palace [where the mayors lived], went to the yearly public assembly of his people to discuss the affairs of the kingdom, and then returned home."

747, after giving away most of his land to the church, Carloman surrendered his noble title and duties as Austrasian mayor of the palace to his brother, Pepin III. Then he traveled to Rome to take the vows of monasticism and retreated to a monastery in Italy. Carloman spent the rest of his life as a devout monk.

Pepin III must have been delighted by these events, for he now became mayor of the palace over the entire kingdom, opening the way to becoming sole master of the kingdom, as his father, Charles Martel, had been. He held vast domains in Austrasia and Neustria and immense power through the vassals who were in his service. He further consolidated his power by assigning the most prestigious church positions in the kingdom to close family allies and wealthy landholders.

Pepin III Becomes the First Carolingian King

Sure of the support of his followers, Pepin III sensed that the hour had come to replace the Merovingian king, Childeric III, and take the throne for himself. Because he held all the real power of the royalty anyway, the decision was quite natural. Still, the mystique of family history was an important aspect of Frankish royalty, so the chroniclers in various monasteries in St. Denis, Metz, and elsewhere began writing so-called official histories of Pepin's ancestors. The accomplishments of Arnulf, his great-great-grandfather, were praised in *The Life of St. Arnulf*. Cults worshiping the miracles of his mother and grandmother appeared, and the great victories of Charles Martel were canonized in

Since family lines were such an important part of Frankish royalty, Pepin III (pictured), glorified his ancestors to justify his claim to the throne.

legend and song. Such efforts made it seem natural that someone whose heritage was so rich in warriors and saints should be a king.

Finally, before having himself elected king of the Franks, Pepin sent Fulrad, one of his appointed bishops, to Rome to consult with Pope Zacharias. Recognizing that Pepin would be a much stronger ally than Childeric, Fulrad counseled Zacharias that "it was better to call him king who had royal power [Pepin] rather than him who did not [Childeric]."[7]

Therefore, in November 751, the young man whom Pepin and his brother had found in a local monastery, to whom they had given the name Childeric III, and whom they had propped up on the

Pepin III Takes the Title of King

The following account of the change from the Merovingian line of kings to the Carolingians is taken from the Annals of Lorsch. *The excerpt quoted here is from Frederick Ogg's* A Source Book of Medieval History. *The year 750, given for Pope Zacharias's declaration, is a mistake, for it did not really occur until 751.*

"In the year 750 of the Lord's incarnation Pepin sent ambassadors to Rome to Pope Zacharias, to inquire concerning the kings of the Franks, who, though they were of the royal line and were called kings, had no power in the kingdom, except that charters and privileges were drawn up in their names. They had absolutely no kingly authority, but did whatever the Major Domus [mayor of the palace] desired. But on the first day of March, according to ancient custom, gifts were offered to these kings by the people, and the king himself sat in the royal seat with the army standing round him and the Major Domus in his presence, and he commanded on that day whatever was decreed by the Franks; but on all other days he remained quietly at home. Pope Zacharias, therefore, in the exercise of his better and more apostolic authority, replied to their inquiry that it seemed to him better and more expedient that the man who held power in the kingdom should be called king and be king, rather than he who falsely bore that name. Therefore, the aforesaid pope commanded the king and people of the Franks that Pepin, who was exercising royal power, should be called king, and should be established on the throne. This was therefore done by the anointing of the holy archbishop Boniface in the city of Soissons. Pepin was proclaimed king, and Childeric, who was falsely called king, was shaved and sent into a monastery."

After being dethroned, Childeric has his hair cut before he is sent to a monastery.

Frankish throne, was sent back to the monastery, and Pepin III became king of the Franks. He was also anointed by the bishops of his realm. This seemingly insignificant act was to have great implications for the politics of Europe for several centuries. Up to this time, the Frankish king had always been a Merovingian, a descendant of Clovis.

Now, Pepin wanted to make certain that only his descendants could rule as kings. As the official documents from his coronation make clear, Pepin was the first Frankish king to insist upon his divine right to be king. The coronation records contain numerous references to "divine Providence having anointed us to the royal throne"; or "with the help of the Lord who placed us on the throne"; and "our elevation to the throne having been wrought wholly through the Lord's help."[8]

The Pope's Anointment of King Pepin

Pepin even called on Pope Stephen II, successor to Pope Zacharias, to travel to St. Denis and repeat the ceremony of anointment. In April 754, the pope re-

Pepin III is carried before Pope Zacharias, who decrees that Pepin should be king. Pepin believed that God anointed him to the throne, and thus he was king by divine right.

anointed not only Pepin but also his two sons, Carloman II and Charles. A monk at the abbey of St. Denis recorded this event and its significance:

> The pious and most flourishing lord Pepin was elevated to the royal throne three years earlier by the authority and order of the lord Pope Zacharias of holy memory, by the unction [anointment] of holy chrism [special oil] received from the hands of the blessed bishops of Gaul, and by the election of all the Franks. Then he was anointed and blessed anew as king and patrician, together with his sons Charles and Carloman, by the hands of Pope Stephen in the church of the martyrs Denis, Rusticus, and Eleutherius, the residence of the venerable abbot and archpriest Fulrad. . . . [Stephen] forbade all, under the threat of . . . excommunication, to dare ever to choose a king from a line other than that of these princes; these whom divine piety had deigned to exalt and confirm by the intercession of the holy apostles and consecrate by the hand of the blessed pontiff [pope], their vicar [deputy].[9]

This was the first time a pope had traveled into what many church leaders called the barbarian lands of north Europe. In addition, his recognition of Pepin III marked the end of official political ties between Rome and the Byzantine Empire and the beginning of a powerful, although often stormy, alliance between Rome and a northern European empire— an alliance that lasted, technically, for over one thousand years.

Stephen's anointment of Pepin III followed lengthy negotiations between the two men. Pope Stephen actually arrived in St. Denis to begin these negotiations in the winter of 753. In return for casting divine authority on the rule of King Pepin, the pope insisted on naming Pepin and his descendants as "patricians," or defenders of Rome. This designation obliged King Pepin to help preserve the church's independence from both the Byzantines and the Lombards. He promised to defend the church's lands as well.

Pepin III Liberates the Church from the Lombards

Meanwhile in Italy, Aistulf, the Lombard king, tried to ward off this new threat from the north by sending a special ambassador to Pepin to present the Lombards' case. The ambassador was none other than Pepin's brother, Carloman, who had been residing for the last six years in an Italian monastery. Pepin coldly refused to meet with his brother and had him arrested and imprisoned in a monastery in Burgundy, where Carloman remained until his death a few months later.

In the spring of 755, Pepin the Short acted on his promise to Pope Stephen II. He led an army to Italy, and a year later, after defeating Aistulf and capturing Pavia, Rome, and a number of other Italian towns, Pepin ordered Abbot Fulrad to lay the keys to Rome and several surrounding towns on the altar of St. Peter's Basilica. These keys symbolized Pepin's gift of this region to the church, and the region became known as the Republic of St. Peter. Ruled by the church as an independent nation, the Republic of St. Peter remained in existence until 1870.

Building the Frankish Kingdom

Having satisfied his obligation to the pope, Pepin turned his attention to regaining control of all the lands that his father had ruled. Each year after 756, Pepin called all of his vassals together for an annual assembly and military campaign. Contemporary accounts of these assemblies show the growing strength of the Carolingian armies and the increased emphasis on cavalries of mounted soldiers, or knights. For example, in 758 an agreement with the Saxons, who formerly paid Pepin five hundred cattle annually, was amended to three hundred horses. Also, Pepin moved the annual military campaigns from March until May to assure the harvest of enough grain to feed the horses.

Along with the growing importance of horses came an emphasis on well-trained knights. Pepin granted fiefs to a growing number of these knights, thereby swelling the ranks of the noble class. The feudal oaths that these knights swore to their lords resembled the one described in the *Royal Frankish Annals*, in which Tassilo of Bavaria swore his loyalty to King Pepin the Short in 757:

> He commended himself into vassalage with his hands, and swore innumerable oaths. Touching the relics of the saints, he promised fealty to King Pepin and his sons Charles and Carloman, behaving honestly and faithfully, in accordance with the law and as a vassal should to his lords.[10]

One region that the Carolingians had long coveted was Aquitaine. The Aquitainians, who still retained some of the civilization and culture of the Roman Empire, had tried fiercely to remain independent from the Carolingians. With their overpowering cavalries and highly organized military campaigns, however, the Franks gradually succeeded in subduing the Aquitainians, but they ruined much of the province in the process. Fields were flattened, towns burned, and monasteries destroyed. The civilization of the region, with its strong ties to classical Rome, had been shattered. Out of fear for their lives, many Aquitainian noblemen swore their allegiance to the raiding Carolingians, but it would take generations to overcome the hatred and distrust that the Aquitainians held for their conquerors.

Increasing Fame

In addition to the conquest of Aquitaine, Pepin led campaigns against Arab colonies in southern France and against Saxon and Frisian barbarians in northern Germany. As Pepin's fame and influence spread, so did the international recognition of the Frankish kingdom, though still remote and barbaric in comparison to the Byzantine and Arab civilizations of the Mediterranean and Near East. Like his predecessors, Pepin did not reside at a single palace; rather, he traveled from one domain to another to live for a time from the produce of each. Pepin's travels were documented by the official charters that he issued from various palaces such as those at Compienge, Ver, Corbeny, Heristal, and Aachen. The official charters also record how the Franks exchanged emissaries with Baghdad, Cordova, Constantinople, and Rome.

Transforming the Royal Government

Pepin also transformed the operation of government. Under the Merovingian kings, and even under Charles Martel, almost all legal activities, such as law enforcement, minting coins, and regulating trade, were in the hands of regional dukes and counts. Pepin was the first Frankish king to regulate these activities on a national level. The following edict is the oldest existing example of a royal charter establishing standard monetary values throughout the Frankish kingdom:

With regard to coinage, we order that no more than twenty-two solidi [a

---

Pope Stephen II Pleads for Help from the Franks

In January 756, Pope Stephen II sent a letter asking Pepin III to defend the church's lands in Italy from the Lombards. The letter, quoted in Pierre Riché's The Carolingians, *is composed as if it were dictated directly by St. Peter.*

"I enjoin you, my adopted sons. . . . Come, snatch my city of Rome from the hands of my enemies along with the people that has been entrusted to me by God. Come, protect the place of my body's repose from the contact of these strangers. Come, deliver the church of God, exposed to the worst torments, the worst oppressions, from the doings of the abominable Lombards. You whom I love so greatly, . . . be sure that among all peoples the Franks are especially dear to me. Thus, I warn and admonish you, most Christian kings, Pepin, Charles, and Carloman; and you of the priestly order, bishops, abbots, priests; and you, dukes and counts; and you, the entire Frankish people—lend credence to my exhortations as though I were living and present before you. For if I am not there in flesh and bones, I am there in spirit."

Pope Stephen II's (pictured) plea for help from Pepin III and the Frankish king's compliance were part of a powerful new alliance between the Roman Church and the Franks.

Pepin stands before the conquered Saxons. Pepin's military campaigns in Saxony, Frisia, and Muslim territories earned him international fame and recognition.

coins] and turn twenty-one solidi to whoever brought the metal.[11]

Charters such as this one became much more common, and much easier to read, during Pepin's reign. The form of the charters themselves, as well as the spelling and use of the Latin language began to improve considerably. In addition, Pepin removed most lay royal administrators and replaced them with clerics who were educated and ordained by the church. The office of mayor of the palace was eliminated, but the other royal offices—everything from royal cupbearer to royal chamberlain (treasurer)—were held almost exclusively by church-trained clerics. This remained a characteristic in the courts of both French and German royalty until the fourteenth century.

Both militarily and politically, Pepin III and Charles Martel laid the foundation for a great Frankish empire. During the summer of 768, Pepin III fell ill, just after his final victory over his opponents in Aquitaine. He died on September 24, 768, at the age of fifty-four. Historians may call him Pepin the Short, but his list of achievements was long. Indeed, the achievements of his son Charlemagne would have been inconceivable without the foundation laid by Charles's father and grandfather.

monetary unit] should be made from a pound-weight [of silver] and that the minter should keep one [solidus of

3 Charlemagne's Kingdom

In keeping with Frankish tradition, Pepin III divided his kingdom between his two sons, assigning one part to his older son, Charles, and the other to his younger son, Carloman. We do not know much about their childhood, but their clashes after both became kings indicate that Charles and his brother did not get along.

We possess only a few facts about Charles's early life before he became king. Even Charles's biographer and close friend, Einhard, claimed that he knew nothing of Charles's youth:

> I consider that it would be foolish for me to write about Charlemagne's birth and childhood, or even about his boyhood, for nothing is set down in writing about this and nobody can be found still alive who claims to have any personal knowledge of these matters.[12]

We do know that at the time of his father's death, Charles was twenty-one, four years older than his brother Carloman. We also know that by this time Charles already had considerable political and military experience. For instance, in January 753, at the age of seven, he had been sent by his father from the royal palace at Ponthion with a small entourage to the nearby town of Langres to welcome Pope Stephen II to Frankia and escort him back to the royal palace. There the pope anointed him and Carloman as heirs to their father's throne and patricians of the church. Frankish annals also show that as a young man, Charles accompanied his father on several military campaigns in Aquitaine.

Perhaps because he was the older and the more experienced brother, Charles inherited the half of the kingdom that included most of Neustria and Austrasia, where the oldest of the family's domains and its most loyal followers were located. His kingdom stretched in an arc from Thuringia to Gascony, completely surrounding Carloman's kingdom on the north and west sides. Charles's half of the kingdom had several strategic advantages. First, most of the noble families in this region had been vassals of the Carolingians for many generations. Second, its borders, with the Atlantic Ocean on one side and Carloman's kingdom on another, were more secure than Carloman's borders with the independent-minded Bavarians and Lombards.

Rebellion in Aquitaine

What Pepin had not foreseen, however, was that Charles and Carloman found it

Charles receives the news of his father's death. Charles and his brother, Carloman, inherited Pepin's kingdom, but since the two did not get along, their shared power was problematic.

impossible to cooperate with each other. Predictably, soon after Pepin's death, the Aquitainians revolted against the new kings and demanded that their original borders be recognized. When Charles and Carloman met to plan their response in 769, they had a serious disagreement, the details of which are unknown. As a result of their disagreement, Carloman led his armies home to Soissons while Charles marched on Aquitaine alone. Thanks to his earlier experiences in Aquitaine, Charles knew his enemy and his territory well. He proved his merit as a commander by successfully putting down the rebellion without any help from Carloman.

Charles now faced a more serious dilemma, though, in patching up the rift with his brother. Time after time, history had shown the Franks that when their various realms allied and cooperated with one another, they were an insurmountable force. When they divided and opposed each other, however, they were no stronger than any number of other European powers, most notably Bavaria and Lombardia, two powerful kingdoms that had become allies through marriages between their royal houses. Charles, who now held little hope of reconciling his differences with Carloman, tried to ally himself with Bavaria and Lombardia, thereby isolating Carloman.

Ironically, the first person to propose these new alliances was Bertrada, the mother of Charles and Carloman. She proposed the alliance not because she favored Charles but because she thought it would keep her two sons from fighting against each other. To secure the new alliances, therefore, she proposed that Charles marry Desiderata, the daughter of the Lombard king, Desiderius. In this way, Charles would become an ally of the Lombards, reinforce his ties to Bavaria, and simultaneously surround his brother with a diplomatic ring.

An Arranged Marriage

When Charles agreed to her plan and married Desiderata in 770, it appeared that Bertrada had achieved what European rulers for the previous three centuries had not: a stable peace. She convinced her two sons to reconcile their

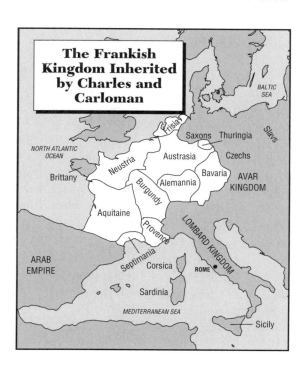

The Frankish Kingdom Inherited by Charles and Carloman

differences and renew their partnership in the rule of Frankia. Both Frankish kings were now allied with the Lombards and the Bavarians.

While these conditions may have seemed ideal to most, they made Charles miserable. The year that followed was perhaps the most trying in all the years of his reign. Today he is remembered as a decisive, self-assured, and ambitious leader, but in 770, as his mother's arrangements unfolded, Charles the Great seemed both personally and politically stifled. For one thing, in order to complete his mother's plan, he had to disown Himiltrude, a woman of common birth who lived with him in an unofficial but happy marriage that produced one son, named Pepin. Both Charles and his new wife, Desiderata, seemed to resent their forced union, and this experience probably influenced Charles's lifelong suspicion of such political marriages. Although numerous marital alliances were later proposed for Charles's daughters, he could never bring himself to approve any of them.

Charles was uncomfortable not only with his new marriage but also with his new allies. His father, Pepin III, had established the Republic of St. Peter for the pope by wresting land from the Lombards. Now Charles found himself in the awkward position of being allied with both the pope and the Lombards. He had inherited the traditions and the policies of his grandfather Charles the Hammer and his father Pepin III, both known for their conquests of Aquitaine, Italy, Burgundy, and Bavaria. Charles wanted conquests of his own. Saxony and Frisia beckoned, as did the call to drive the Moors back beyond the Pyrenees. Yet, his hands were tied. Forced to consult his brother and the rulers of other realms, Charles was neutralized. Although the web of alliances spun by his mother brought peace to Europe, Charles felt as trapped as a fly in a spider's web.

Charles Breaks Up the Alliance

Quite suddenly, in 771 Charles made a bold decision that simultaneously threw Europe back into a state of turmoil and thrust him into the forefront of the turbulence, where he would remain for the next forty years. He divorced Desiderata and sent her back to her father, effectively canceling his alliance with the Lombards and weakening his ties with Bavaria. At the same time, he married a Frankish woman, Hildegard, who was cheerful and vigorous and proved to be the partner Charles needed.

Although these rash steps upset the peaceful balance among the Lombards, Bavarians, and Franks, the effect they had on Charles can only be described as positive. From an uncertain, immature, young king who relied on the judgments of others, he emerged confident, decisive, self-assured, and defiant. True to his heritage, Charles made a better leader than a follower. He proved brighter, more convincing, and happier as an aggressive leader

Charlemagne's First Marriage

As George Philip Baker explains in Charles and the United States of Europe, *Charlemagne's first marriage was an "unofficial" bond, which demonstrates the modified version of monogamy practiced by many Frankish noblemen.*

"Nothing in the customs of the Franks—nor in those of any North-European people—tied Charles for ever to Himiltrud [sic]. He was quite at liberty to break the bond when a good reason could be given for doing so. The conception of the indissoluble monogamous marriage had not yet penetrated to the world in which Charles lived, nor did Charles himself ever accept such a doctrine. The binding quality of a marriage varied somewhat according to the status of the parties. Some day, perhaps, Charles would marry a wife of birth equal to his own, with a vast dowry—and this would be a bond far harder to break. As for Himiltrud, when the time came, her dowry would be returned and perhaps a pension paid her—and every one would be satisfied.

This first marriage of Charles was part of his apprenticeship. He was learning; and he was not expected to make any binding engagements yet."

than as a passive one. Although he angered other rulers and risked war with them, he preferred being his own man to following the counsel of others.

Among those whom Charles had angered, of course, was Desiderius, the Lombard king. Marrying a woman and then returning her to her father is never well received, especially by a king. Desiderius was incensed by this insult, and he threatened to invade Charles's kingdom in alliance with Carloman and Carloman's friends in Burgundy and Provence. Threats and rumors of war flew like arrows between the Lombard and Frankish kingdoms.

The Death of Carloman: Charles Becomes King over All of Frankia

Then, very suddenly, in December 771, the threats and rumors stopped. The reason: Charles's brother Carloman died suddenly at the age of twenty. Overnight, the troublesome division of the Frankish kingdom disappeared as Charles announced that he was annexing his brother's kingdom. Carloman's widow, Gerberga, claimed the kingdom for their two sons and proclaimed herself as their regent, or official supervisor. With few exceptions, however, the vassals and allies who had been loyal to Carloman while he lived now proclaimed their loyalty to Charles. Without the support of her husband's strongest vassals, Gerberga realized that her protests were hopeless, so she fled with her two sons to the court of Desiderius in Pavia, Italy, and proclaimed herself regent in exile. Although she posed no immediate

When Carloman died suddenly, Charles (pictured) annexed his brother's kingdom to his own and began his reign as sole ruler of the Frankish kingdom.

threat to Charles, her asylum with Desiderius further weakened the ties between the Franks and the Lombards.

The death of Carloman was one of those odd coincidences that so often change the direction of history. The sudden death of Carloman transformed Charles's future from one of peril to one of opportunity. Few men, of his age or any other, could have seized the opportunity as decisively and built upon it as convincingly as Charles did.

Einhard, Charles's Confidant and Biographer

The most complete picture of Charlemagne comes from the biography written shortly after his death by his adviser and close friend Einhard. In part, we also have

Einhard (pictured) was a close friend and adviser to Charlemagne. Einhard's biography Two Lives of Charlemagne *provides much direct, if one-sided, information about the Frankish king.*

building and policing roads that linked important trade cities and royal domains. In his Introduction to *Two Lives of Charlemagne*, Einhard writes of "the friendly relations which I enjoyed with [Charles] and his children from the moment when I first began to live at his court."[13]

Although Einhard said little more than this about himself in his biography of Charles, official annals of Charles's reign as king mention that Einhard was once entrusted as an emissary to Pope Leo III. Other obscure records from the Fulda monastery suggest that he supervised "public works" within the kingdom and taught "the arts." According to the abbot of Reichenau, Charles trusted no adviser more than he trusted Einhard.

A Portrait of the Young King

Einhard has given us a fairly intimate portrait of Charles's private life and personality as well as an account of his accomplishments as a king and emperor. Of course, the biography carefully selects and describes events to present Charles in the best possible light. For example, he omits any discussion of Charles's relationship with his brother Carloman, and he barely mentions Charles's first (unofficial) marriage, to Himiltrude or his second, to Desiderata. This is to be expected from a biographer who enjoyed the lifelong rewards of friendship with the king. In fact, Einhard states that his purpose in writing the biography was to describe

the extraordinary life of this most remarkable king, the greatest man of all

Charles himself to thank for the preservation of this biography, for it was his own love and support of classical learning and literature that led to the creation of libraries like the one at Fulda where Einhard was educated and later returned to write his *Vita Caroli*, or *Two Lives of Charlemagne*. Einhard modeled his biography on the work of a Latin author, Suetonius, whose *De Vita Caesarum*, or *The Lives of the Caesars*, Einhard found at the monastery in Fulda.

Einhard was an extremely well educated man of noble birth whose parents helped support the monastery at Fulda where Einhard was educated. In 791 or 792 he was sent from Fulda to Charles's Palace School at Aachen, in what is now northern Germany. A man of many talents, Einhard soon caught the king's attention and was put in charge of administering many public works, such as those living in his own period, . . . together with his outstanding achievements, which can scarcely be matched by modern men.[14]

It is especially to be expected knowing that Charles's son and successor, Louis the Pious, made Einhard a wealthy abbot and landholder during the time that Einhard was writing *Two Lives of Charlemagne*.

Einhard describes Charles physically as a tall, strong, well-built man with flowing white hair, "and his eyes were piercing and unusually large." His expression was normally "gay and good-humoured." Despite being "a trifle too heavy, . . . [he] always appeared masterful and dignified, . . . preventing one from noticing these blemishes. His step was firm and he was manly in all his movements."[15]

Charles ate and drank moderately and "was so sparing in his use of wine and every other beverage that he rarely drank more than three times in the course of his dinner." Einhard's description of the atmosphere and activities that surrounded Charles's meals give us greater insight into his character:

> He rarely gave banquets and these only on high feast days, but then he would invite a great number of guests. His main meal of the day was served in four courses, in addition to the roast meat which his hunters used to bring in on spits and which he enjoyed more

Charlemagne's Wives and Concubines

In the following excerpt from Two Lives of Charlemagne, *Einhard identifies the king's several wives and matter-of-factly acknowledges his numerous concubines.*

"At the bidding of his mother, he married the daughter of Desiderius, the King of the Longobards. Nobody knows why, but he dismissed this wife after one year. Next he married Hildigard, a woman of most noble family, from the Swabian race. By her he had three sons, Charles, Pepin, and Lewis, and the same number of daughters, Rotrude, Bertha, and Gisela. He had three more daughters, Theoderada, Hiltrude, and Rothaide, two of these by his third wife, Fastrada, who was from the race of Eastern Franks or Germans, and the last by a concubine whose name I cannot remember. Fastrada died and he married Luitgard, from the Alemanni, but she bore him no children. After Luitgard's death, he took four concubines: Madelgard, who bore him a daughter Ruothilde; Gersvinda, of the Saxon race, by whom he had a daughter Adaltrude; Regina, who bore him Drogo and Hugo; and Adallinda, who become the mother of Theodoric."

than any other food. During his meal he would listen to a public reading or some other entertainment. Stories would be recited for him, or the doings of the ancients told again. He took great pleasure in the books of Saint Augustine and especially in those which are called *The City of God*.[16]

He seems to have been what we would now call very down-to-earth. Einhard tells us that Charles's preferred style of dress "differed hardly at all from that of the common people." Again, Einhard's simple, eloquent description tells us far more about the man than simply what clothes he wore:

He wore the national dress of the Franks. Next to his skin he had a linen shirt and linen drawers; and then long hose and a tunic edged with silk. He wore shoes on his feet and bands of cloth wound round his legs. In winter he protected his chest and shoulders with a jerkin [vest] made of otter skins and ermine.

He wrapped himself in a blue cloak and always had a sword strapped to his side, with a hilt and belt of gold or silver. Sometimes he would use a jewelled sword, but this was only on great feast days or when ambassadors came from foreign peoples. He hated the clothes

Charles stands behind the table at his court while food and drinks are served. He appears to have avoided excessive eating and drinking himself, and he rarely held banquets.

Charlemagne (top right corner) mourns the deaths of his knights in battle. During his monarchy, he dressed simply, avoiding grandiose, ornate outfits.

of other countries, no matter how becoming they might be, and he would never consent to wear them. . . . On feast days he walked in procession in a suit of cloth of gold, with jewelled shoes, his cloak fastened with a golden brooch and with a crown of gold and precious stones on his head. On ordinary days his dress differed hardly at all from that of the common people."[17]

As we begin to form a mental picture of this Frankish king, it comes as little surprise that he loved outdoor activity of all kinds:

He spent much of his time on horseback and out hunting, which came naturally to him, for it would be difficult to find another race on earth who could equal the Franks in this activity. He took delight in steam-baths at the thermal springs, and loved to exercise himself in the water whenever he could. He was an extremely strong swimmer and in this sport no one could surpass him. It was for this reason that he built his palace at Aachen and remained continuously in residence there during the last years of his life and indeed until the moment of his death. He would invite not only his sons to bathe with him, but his nobles and friends as well, and occasionally

Charles (left) listens as a subject reads to him. Coordinating with subordinates in his vast kingdom required extensive travel, and Charles, being greatly attached to his children, brought them along on the journeys.

even a crowd of his attendants and bodyguards, so that sometimes a hundred men or more would be in the water together.[18]

Einhard also describes his king as a deeply devoted and loving father:

He paid such attention to the upbringing of his sons and daughters that he never sat down to table without them

when he was at home, and never set out on a journey without taking them with him. His sons rode at his side and his daughters followed along behind. Hand-picked guards watched over them as they closed the line of march. These girls were extraordinarily beautiful and greatly loved by their father. It is a remarkable fact that, as a result of this, he kept them with him in his household until the very day of his death, instead of giving them in marriage to his own men or to foreigners, maintaining that he could not live without them.[19]

Charles apparently held deep feelings for his personal friends. Einhard says:

When the death of Hadrian, the Pope of Rome and his close friend, was announced to him, he wept as if he had lost a brother or a dearly loved son. He was firm and steady in his human relationships, developing friendship easily, keeping it up with care and doing everything he possibly could for anyone whom he had admitted to this degree of intimacy.[20]

Einhard also describes Charles as a gracious host:

He loved foreigners and took great pains to make them welcome. So many visited him as a result that they were rightly held to be a burden not only to the palace, but to the entire realm. In his magnanimity [generosity] he took no notice at all of this criticism, for he considered that his reputation for hospitality and the advantage of the good name which he acquired more than compensated for the great nuisance of their being there.[21]

Einhard also goes to great lengths to describe Charles's passion for learning, but he emphasizes that Charles did not envision the well-educated nobleman as an idle thinker. He was a great soldier and horseman and also trained and groomed his own horses. He insisted that his children—both sons and daughters—learn practical, manual skills as well as the liberal arts:

Charles was determined to give his children, his daughters just as much as his sons, a proper training in the liberal arts which had formed the subject of his own studies. As soon as they were old enough he had his sons taught to ride in the Frankish fashion, to use arms and to hunt. He made his daughters learn to spin and weave wool, use the distaff and spindle, and acquire every womanly accomplishment, rather than fritter away their time in sheer idleness.[22]

Underlying Charles's passion for learning was a vision of a new Christian

Foreign visitors offer gifts to Charles. The king had a reputation as a gracious host, and he welcomed guests to Frankia with hospitality and generosity.

civilization, one in which all his subjects— not just the nobility—were uplifted in mind and spirit. Central to this vision was the role of the church, which in the age of Charles was the torchbearer of culture and enlightenment as well as salvation. That is why, Einhard explains, he cared more about and did more for the church than he did even for his own family. Finally, he assures us that Charles's religious fervor carried over to acts of Christian charity:

> He was most active in relieving the poor and in that form of really disinterested charity which the Greeks call *eleemosyna*. He gave alms not only in his own country and in the kingdom over which he reigned, but also across the sea in Syria, Egypt, Africa, Jerusalem, Alexandria, and Carthage. Wherever he heard that Christians were living in want, he took pity on their poverty and sent them money regularly. It was, indeed, precisely for this reason that he sought the friendship of kings beyond the sea, for he hoped that some relief and alleviation might result for the Christians living under their domination.[23]

How Accurate Is Einhard's Biography?

Of course, we know that Einhard's view of Charles is one-sided. We know that this same Charles loved to hear the cry of battle, and in answering that cry, he could be bloodthirsty and vengeful. In general, however, we must take Einhard at his word: Charles was an extraordinary individual who inspired deep admiration

This engraving depicts Charlemagne worshiping the Virgin Mary and Jesus. Christianity was a vital part of Charlemagne's rule; he saw it as the way to salvation and enlightenment for all of his subjects.

Charlemagne's Devotion to the Church

Despite his unusual views regarding marriage, Charlemagne "practiced the Christian religion with great devotion and piety," at least according to Einhard.

"As long as his health lasted he went to church morning and evening with great regularity, and also for early-morning Mass, and the late-night hours. He took the greatest pains to ensure that all church ceremonies were performed with the utmost dignity, and he was always warning the sacristans to see that nothing sordid or dirty was brought into the building or left there. He donated so many sacred vessels made of gold and silver, and so many priestly vestments, that when service time came even those who opened and closed the doors, surely the humblest of all church dignitaries, had no need to perform their duties in their everyday clothes.

He made careful reforms in the way in which the psalms were chanted and the lessons read. He was himself quite an expert at both of these exercises, but he never read the lesson in public and he would sing only with the rest of the congregation and then in a low voice."

among most of his subjects. Perhaps what is remarkable about Charles is not that a man of such learning and civility could also be a barbarous, bloodthirsty killer, but that in such a barbarous and bloodthirsty age, a warrior king could also care so deeply about his subjects and about the life of the mind and the soul. Perhaps Einhard's portrait of Charles, complete with its contradictions and obvious embellishments, can help us understand the reverence that Charlemagne's contemporaries felt for this great commander, king, and emperor.

4 Expanding the Frankish Kingdom

Charles's grandfather Charles Martel and his father Pepin III were the first Frankish leaders since Clovis to assert their authority over the nobility. During the reigns of the Merovingian kings, the noblemen had ruled their lands independently. They controlled their kings rather than vice versa; the role of the Merovingian king was restricted to organizing armies of Frankish noblemen against foreign powers, such as the Moors, Lombards, or Saxons.

The King as Commander in Chief

In fact, Charles Martel and Pepin III had become more powerful than their Merovingian predecessors because they kept their Frankish armies organized and active. Their aggressive foreign policy helped to ensure their domestic control. Charlemagne learned from them, and he applied this lesson in working toward his goal of building a powerful central government in the style of the Romans. He despised local noblemen who challenged the authority of his government. He believed his authority had been granted to him by God, but in practice, he controlled the local Frankish lords by keeping them at war against foreign threats—real or imagined. As many historians have observed, Charles's reign was one continuous military campaign.

Like his father, Charles combined the annual general assembly of noblemen with a military campaign. All the noblemen in the kingdom were required by law to attend these assemblies, where they would discuss the king's proposals for taxes, punishing crimes, penalizing vassals who deserted their lords, and so forth. They submitted their suggestions to Charles, who formulated those he approved of as *capitula*, or laws. The sixty-five capitularies, or written collections of laws, that have been preserved provide a fairly complete record of Charles's government.

Although the capitularies show the political importance of the general assemblies, decrees like the following, sent from Charles to Abbot Fulrad, demonstrate how Charles also used the general assembly to begin his annual military campaigns:

Be it known to you that we shall hold our general assembly this year in eastern Saxony. . . . Wherefore we command you to be present there on 17 June with your men well armed and equipped. . . . You should come with whatever arms, implements, provision, and clothing may be needed to proceed from there with the army to whichever region we shall command. Each horseman should have a shield, a spear, a long-sword and a short-sword, a bow, a quiver, and arrows. Your carts should contain implements for various purposes. . . . There should also be provisions for three months, and weapons and clothing for six. . . . Your men should proceed to the appointed place by the shortest route, commandeering nothing along the way except for grass, firewood, and water.[24]

Through a century of Frankish expansion under the Carolingians, many Frankish counts expanded both their landholdings and the size of their armies. To keep their knights loyal, the counts gave the knights land as fiefs. As landholders who ruled over one or more villages, these knights joined the ranks of the nobility and swore fealty oaths to their respective lords.

In addition to these oaths, Charles required every single landowner in the kingdom to swear an oath of allegiance to him.

The Conquests of Charles the Great

In Two Lives of Charlemagne, *Einhard summarizes Charles's conquests and describes the boundaries of the Frankish kingdom before and after Charles's reign.*

"Such were the wars that this all-powerful king fought during the 47 years of his reign in various parts of the world with as much prudence as good fortune. Thus, the Frankish realm, which his father, Pepin, left to him already vast and powerful, emerged from his glorious hands almost doubled in size. Before him—excepting the dependent lands of Alemannia and Bavaria—this kingdom included only the part of Gaul situated between the Rhine, the Loire, the Ocean, the Baltic Sea, and the part of Germany inhabited by the so-called eastern Franks—that is, between Saxony, the Danube, the Rhine, and the Saale, which separates Thuringia from the land of the Sorbs. After the wars which we have described Charles added Aquitaine, Gascony, the entire range of the Pyrenees, and the lands up to the Ebro River. . . . To this he added Italy, which extends for over a million paces from Aosta to lower Calabria and the border between the Beneventans and the Greeks. He added the two Pannonian provinces, Dacia, Istri, Liburnia, Dalmatia. . . . Finally, between the Rhine, the Atlantic, the Vistula and Danube, he tamed and subjected all the barbarian and savage peoples of Germany."

As specified in one of his capitularies, the exact words of the oath were these: "I declare and promise without fraud and malice that I am, and will be, faithful to my lord King Charles, and his sons, all the days of my life."[25] The consequences of breaking this starkly simple oath were well understood throughout the kingdom. As a result, Charles had a huge army at his beck and call. When he called his counts to battle, they called their vassals, who, in turn, called vassals of their own. As a result, great cavalries of highly skilled knights would arrive from every corner of the kingdom. Although many noblemen complained bitterly about their military obligations, called the *heerbann*, few dared to defy them.

Charles figured out in exact detail what each freeman in his kingdom was required to contribute to the *heerbann* and what fines to exact upon those who did not meet their obligation. Every freeman owed the king three months of military service,

or its equivalent, each year. If a citizen lived close to the designated site of the military campaign, he was required to appear in person and to provide his own weapons and three months' worth of food and supplies. If the campaign was targeted on a foreign land some distance away, poorer freemen were relieved of their obligation to appear in person, but they had to contribute between one-sixth and one-half of a knight's expenses, depending on their relative wealth, which was measured by the amount of land they held. In the classic *A History of Charles the Great*, written in 1888, Jacob Mombert summarizes the process of calling a great assembly:

> When the king had resolved upon some military expedition, he sent his *missi* [emissaries] throughout the realm to summon the *heerbann*, requiring all free men to assemble on a given day and at a set place . . .; those who came too late were fined; their

A noble proclaims an oath of allegiance to Charlemagne. As subjects of the king, nobles were obligated to perform three months of military service each year, called the heerbann.

equipment in arms consisted of a sword, a shield, and a lance, or where no lance was brought, a bow with two strings and twelve arrows was accepted in its place.

The owner of twelve mansi [a measurement of land] had to furnish a cuirass [armor made of leather] and a helmet; failure to supply either imperilled his fief. Owners of landed property on the line of march were bound to furnish transportation for the personal effects and provisions of the king, the court, the bishops, abbots, and counts. The counts were held responsible for good roads and bridges, and were not slow to impose this additional burden on the long-suffering country population; the troops were quartered upon [housed by] the people; and the counts, moreover, expressly enjoined to reserve two-thirds of the grass and hay in their counties, so that the horses and cattle of the entire army might be fed.[26]

Charles's First Venture into Saxony

The land that Charles longed to subdue above all others was Saxony. This northern German home of the Saxon people had resisted colonization and Christianization since the time of the Romans. The Saxons still worshiped Othin, the Germanic tree god, which Charles, who saw himself an enlightened Christian, despised. Warning

Charlemagne orders the sacred tree of the Saxons, the Irminsul, *cut down. Charlemagne destroyed the tree after the Saxons continued to worship it, refusing to accept Christianity.*

his people that if they did not invade Saxony, the Saxons would invade other Frankish allies whose lands bordered on Saxony, he organized his first Saxon campaign in the summer of 772.

Charles marched as far east into Saxony as the city of Paderborn, where he made his intentions clear by cutting down the *Irminsul*, or holy tree, one of the chief religious objects of Saxony, and seizing the treasures from the Saxon temple. His Saxon campaign was cut short, however, by desperate cries for help from allies closer to home. Pope Hadrian sent messengers to Charles in Saxony, notifying him that the Lombards, still ruled by Desiderius, were threatening to take back most of the Republic of St. Peter in Italy, which Pepin had donated to the church.

A Race to Italy

The following spring, Charles led his armies on an arduous march across the Alps and into northern Italy. When the Franks neared the Italian city of Turin,

Charles displayed some of his military cunning by dividing his forces into two armies. Charles led the larger army himself, and his uncle, Bernhard, led the other. When Desiderius intercepted Charles's division near Turin, he had every confidence that he had trapped the Frankish king in a mountain pass.

Charles even encouraged this perception, offering to negotiate a sale of the papal claims. As intended, Desiderius interpreted the offer as a sign of weakness and refused to consider it. When Desiderius began to close ranks on Charles's army, however, he was completely surprised by Bernhard's army, which attacked him from the rear. Then, when Desiderius's army turned to fight Bernhard, Charles led his army out of the trap and directly toward Pavia, the Lombard capital. Realizing that he had to defend Pavia, Desiderius retreated from battle and raced back to the capital.

The Siege of Pavia, 773–774

Desiderius reached Pavia just ahead of Charles, forcing the Franks to lay siege to Pavia. They surrounded the city so that no one could enter or exit. This was not the first time the Franks had attempted to take Pavia by siege, however, and the people of Pavia were ready. The city was heavily fortified, and the residents were well supplied with stores of food.

A century and a half later, a besieging army would have employed siege towers, catapults, crossbows, tunnels, and other equipment to attack the fortified city. However, in 773 the Franks did not know these feats of engineering. Nevertheless,

Charles's army was carefully organized, well disciplined, and well supplied with food and clothing. The Pavians may have been ready for a siege, but not one that lasted through the winter. The spring of 774 found the Lombards still holed up inside of Pavia; the Franks were patiently surrounding the city, waiting like vultures.

Charles's First Visit to Rome

Charles was so confident of the eventual success of his siege that he decided to make an Easter visit to Rome. It was his first trip to Rome and his first personal audience with the new pope, Hadrian. Having just rescued the church's land, Charles held a favorable bargaining position, but he made no additional demands on the church. He simply reconfirmed the donation of Pepin III, and Hadrian agreed that all other lands the Franks captured from the Lombards should be considered fair spoils of war.

Charles's visit with Hadrian had several important, lasting results. For one thing, it led to a lifelong friendship between Charles and Hadrian. The effect this friendship had on binding the Frankish nobility and the Roman church and the effects of that relationship on the history of Europe can scarcely be overestimated. This was the first of four visits that Charles would make to the city of Rome. It was a long and difficult journey in those days, but Charles had fallen in love with Rome and its traditions. As Einhard tells us, Charles pledged to restore Rome to its original glory and prestige as the capital of the great Roman Empire:

Charles cared more for the church of the holy Apostle Peter in Rome than for any other sacred and venerable place. He poured into its treasury a vast fortune in gold and silver coinage and in precious stones. He sent so many gifts to the Pope that it was impossible to keep count of them. Throughout the whole period of his reign nothing was ever nearer to his heart than that, by his own efforts and exertion, the city of Rome should regain its former proud position.[27]

Charles Becomes King of the Lombards

Meanwhile, Desiderius continued to hold out in Pavia until the summer of 774. When Desiderius finally surrendered, Charles exiled him to a monastery in Neustria and spared the lives of his defenders. He had himself crowned as king of the Lombards, but he did not try to annex Lombardia into the Frankish kingdom. Instead, he recognized Lombardia as a separate state and allowed the Lombard nobility to govern themselves as long as they provided military assistance to him when he called upon them to do so. Each Lombard nobleman was ordered to swear homage to Charles, and only Arichis, the duke of Benevento, refused.

Charles let this matter of insubordination pass for the moment. In fact, he seemed content with the state of affairs in Italy and hastened to return to Saxony. Over the next twenty-five years, Charles the Great would wage wars as far east as modern-day Hungary and as far west as Spain, but he conducted most of his bat-

tles in either Lombardia or Saxony. Charles's treatment of these two enemies is as strikingly different as the geographical differences between the green hills of Lombardia in northern Italy and the cold Saxon flatlands along the Baltic Sea.

The Lombards were not natural enemies of the Franks. In fact, both nations had adopted many of the same customs from the Romans. They shared the same religion, many of the same laws, and similar legal systems. Many members of the Lombard and Frankish nobility had even intermarried. Thus, Charles never intended to conquer and change the entire culture in Lombardia, but simply to quell the small groups of rebel noblemen whose ambitions clashed with his own. Charles's wars with these ambitious noblemen were feudal wars, essentially wars between competitors within the same social and economic framework.

The Saxons, on the other hand, had long been natural enemies of the Franks. They represented the old Germanic tribal culture from which the Franks had evolved. Both the Franks and the Saxons had migrated west from northern and central Europe during the time of the Great Migration in the third through the fifth centuries. No significant geographical boundaries separated them, so they had often fought for the same land.

More than anything else, though, Charles regarded the Saxons as barbarians and as enemies of the Christian-Roman-Frankish civilization, which he believed he was destined to build. He believed it was his responsibility to conquer barbaric frontiers and savage peoples, much like the Romans had. The savages that Charles sought to conquer were the Saxons, with their tribal religion and culture. Although not

A Lombard. Charlemagne crowned himself king of Lombardia, but he did not annex the kingdom to his own. Instead, he allowed the Lombards to have a separate state and rule themselves, provided that they swore homage to him.

really a threat to the existing frontiers of civilization in Gaul and Italy, they stood in the way of expanding those frontiers. In his biography of Charles, Einhard summarizes the popular attitude toward the Saxons:

> The Saxons, like almost all the peoples living in Germany, are ferocious by nature. They are much given to devil worship and they are hostile to our religion. They think it no dishonour to violate and transgress the laws of God and man. Hardly a day passed without some incident or other which was well calculated to break the peace. Our borders and theirs were contiguous and nearly everywhere in flat, open country, except, indeed, for a few places where great forest or mountain ranges interposed to separate the territories of the two peoples by a clear demarcation line. Murder, robbery and arson were of constant occurrence on both sides. In the end, the Franks were so irritated by these incidents that they decided that the time had come to abandon retaliatory measures and to undertake a full-scale war against these Saxons.[28]

Resuming the Saxon Campaign

In the spring of 775, as soon as the weather permitted, Charles began his second Saxon campaign. Marching north and east through the region known as Westphalia, he reached the Weser River with little confrontation. The Saxons were ill prepared for Charles's enormous armies, which swept through their fields of grain like swarms of locusts. The much smaller Saxon armies, organized around local clan leaders, were powerless to resist such a pestilence.

Wherever Charles marched in Saxony, he made two demands: that the clan leaders receive Christian baptism and that they swear homage to him. Hessi, chief of Saxon Eastphalia, was the first to perform these two necessary acts, and the Eastphalian

Charles had converted the Saxons in Westphalia to Christianity, but when he discovered that they had not truly embraced the new religion and continued to worship their own gods, he tore down their pagan temples.

nobility followed his example. Charles rewarded Hessi by naming him duke of Eastphalia and proclaiming that all local chiefs must swear their fealty to him. By such acts, Charles hoped to abolish the local tribal organization and transform it into a Frankish feudal system.

As Charles marched back through Westphalia, he discovered that many of the Saxons had not taken their baptism se-riously and continued to worship their Germanic gods. An angry Charles burned temples and wheat fields, and he took several thousand hostages—mostly children—whom he promised to return once their families demonstrated their sincere allegiance to the Christian God and Charles, his Frankish vicar. Charles kept his word, first sending most hostages to monasteries to receive a Christian education and then sending them back to their native lands to convert their people.

Witikind Leads the Saxon Revolt

Charles's first Saxon campaign had been deceptively easy. The resistance attempted by individual clans could not match the Franks' huge, well-organized army. The following spring, however, in the year 776, several Saxon chieftains, led by the chieftain Witikind, organized their own army from several clans and attacked the Frankish fortresses in Saxony, which Charles had left under the protection of small Frankish armies. This time, the shoe was on the other foot; the Franks were outnumbered and severely defeated. At the city of Eresburg, for instance, the Saxons overtook the Frankish fortress and slaughtered most of the soldiers who

A Saxon leader surveys his army. As small, separate clans, the Saxons were powerless to resist the Franks, but the tables were turned when the Saxons united under one chieftain in 776.

were stationed there. Then they laid siege to another Frankish fortress at Sigiburg.

Charles was in Italy when he received word of the fall of Eresburg. Riding night and day, he crossed the Alps, marched up the Rhine River valley, and arrived at the besieged fortress of Sigiburg weeks before anyone expected him. He ordered that the grain fields around the fortress be set on fire.

Charles's sudden appearance shocked the Saxons. Convinced that he must have had supernatural powers to get from Italy to Saxony so fast, most of them forsook Witikind and surrendered to Charles. With the remains of his army, Witikind retreated to Denmark. After reinforcing the fortress at Eresburg and building a new fortress at the city of Karlstadt, Charles returned to Austrasia for the winter.

The Official Annexation of Saxony at the Paderborn Assembly, 777

Although the Saxons had been subdued once again, Charles now realized that small garrisons of knights at fortresses scattered across the occupied regions of Saxony could not defend themselves against interclan alliances of Saxons. He could never hope to transform Saxony and bring it into the fold of civilized states unless he established a more permanent presence there. To that end, Charles called for the Frankish general assembly of 777 to be held in the spring at the Saxon capital of Paderborn. Frankish counts from Austrasia, Neustria, Brittany, Burgundy, and Aquitaine came to Paderborn on large steeds, bedecked with ar-

mor and blankets bearing their respective colors and coats of arms. The noblemen wore their families' colors and crests on their mantles, mail coats, and cone-shaped helmets. They were followed by knights mounted on horseback, carrying long swords, lances, and the banners of their respective lords. Behind the knights walked thousands of foot soldiers, carrying bows, axes, shovels, and other weapons and tool. Following in the distance were wagons loaded with provisions and building supplies. These enormous processions were a frightening show of force to the Saxons who watched their conquerors march through their fields, raising huge clouds of dust that could be seen for miles.

At Paderborn, Charles proclaimed that he was officially annexing Saxony as part of the Frankish kingdom. He divided the conquered regions of Saxony into several duchies, and he stripped the traditional tribal leaders of their power. Charles redistributed the conquered regions to the leaders who accepted baptism and swore oaths of allegiance to him and assigned them titles of duke, count, or viscount. He demanded that these noblemen set aside lands for Christian churches and monasteries. To underscore the fact that Saxony was now part of the Frankish kingdom, Charles built an eastern palace at Paderborn, using Saxon peasants and prisoners of war as slave labor.

The first Council of Paderborn in 777 was even attended by foreign emissaries. The appearance of several turbaned, dark-skinned, Moorish chiefs must have startled many Saxons, especially when they learned that their new king had invited the Moors to come to Paderborn. The Moors were enemies of the current Moorish caliph in

At the Council of Paderborn in 777, Moorish emissaries ask for Charles's help in overthrowing the caliph of Islamic Spain.

Spain, and they came to request Charles's aid in overthrowing their ruler.

The Rising Prestige and Military Power of Charles the Great

The heart of Saxony seems an unlikely spot in which to plan a military alliance with Moors from Spain. The great Moorish civilization lay beyond the rugged Pyrenees, west and south of the Franks' southernmost territories in Aquitaine. The Moors had conquered much of Spain and, over the course of two centuries, had built a prosperous, highly advanced Muslim civilization there.

Like the Franks, they built their military success around cavalries of mounted soldiers. Stories of the legendary Spanish knight El Cid come from this age when Moors and their Arabian horses were thought to possess magical speed and stamina. The Moors' art of horsemanship was a sign of their prosperity. Supporting armies of horsemen, with their need for special weapons, equipment, and stables of horses, required a certain level of prosperity and stability. From the time of Charles Martel, the Franks, too, had used their rising prosperity to establish a military built around cavalries of well-trained and well-equipped knights.

Charles Martel's armies had held their ground in Aquitaine against raiding cavalries of Moors, but they had never tried to cross over the Pyrenees and defeat the Moors on their homeland. Later, under Pepin III and Charles the Great, the Franks crossed the Alps and defeated the

A Capitula Concerning Military Service

Charles's ironclad capitularies concerning mandatory military service specified precisely what each person's obligations were and the punishments for failing to meet them. The following capitula *was summarized by Jacob Mombert in* A History of Charles the Great.

"The capitula recites:

1. That every freeman is liable to military service and in the event of failure, subject to a fine of sixty *solidi*, or the loss of his liberty if he cannot pay the fine; the payment of the fine restores him to freedom; death alone annuls the obligation.

2. That two-thirds of the [fine] are payable to the sovereign, one-third to the count. Gold, silver, clothes, arms, game, and cattle are legal tender, but land and slaves are not legal tender, in payment of the fine.

3. That delinquent vassals, tardy in responding to the call for field service, are to undergo the punishment of subsisting on bread and water only for as many days as they are late.

4. That the crime of . . . desertion from before the enemy is to be a capital offence.

5. That refusal of a vassal to serve with his equal to be punished with the loss of his fief.

6. An absolute ban against drinking before the enemy. Inebriates in the army to be put on water."

Lombards. And in 777, Charles was able to quell a Lombard revolt on one side of the Alps and appear almost miraculously on the other side two weeks later.

Charles called his noblemen knights, or professional soldiers who specialized in horsemanship. In fact, the French word for knight, which originated in this period, is *chevallier*, which means "horseman." These knights, or horsemen, made it possible for Charles, while holding court in the distant Saxon city of Paderborn, to decide upon a course of action that neither Charles Martel nor Pepin III could have contemplated: a Frankish invasion of Spain.

Roland and the Legendary Spanish Campaign

Throughout the winter of 777–778, Charles prepared for his Spanish campaign while his *missi* enthusiastically spread the word of the impending march. The remarkable Muslim conquests of the seventh and eighth centuries inspired a mixture of fear and admiration among the Franks. The Arabs, with their superior horses and horsemanship, had expanded almost at will in every direction, conquering virtually the whole of northern Africa and most of Spain. In many ways the triumphs of the Moors resembled those of the Franks themselves. The confrontation between the Franks and the Moors, then, promised to be a showdown of the two mightiest mounted forces in Europe.

The showdown in the Pyrenees between Charles's Christian warriors and the Saracens, or infidels, has become legendary. It is recalled in *The Song of Roland*, one of the most famous epic poems of Western literature. The poem tells the story of the death of Roland, one of Charlemagne's heroic vassals, whose self-sacrifice for the good of his countrymen makes a grand story of courage and loyalty. Unfortunately, the decisive battles and heroic sacrifices recorded in *The Song of Roland* are fictitious. They are based on a minor skirmish between the rear guard of Charles's army and a band of Basques, not Moors as *The Song of Roland* claims.

The Basques were a tribe of people native to the Pyrenees. Far from being Moors or even allies of the Moors, the Basques probably had more reason to hate and fear the Moors than did the Franks. In fact, there is no historical evidence that Charles's armies ever engaged in any battles with the Moors on this campaign.

The southward march began sometime after Christmas of 777, which Charles spent at his domain on the Meuse River, near the modern border between France and Belgium. As was the Frankish custom at this time, Charles had no permanently located court. Wherever he went, his court went with him, from domain to domain and even from campaign to campaign. According to legend, Charles surrounded himself with the twelve bravest and brightest men in his kingdom, who became known as his paladins, or chosen knights. Although the term *paladin* and their exact number

The Song of Roland *is an epic poem about a battle in the Pyrenees. This scene depicts the death of Roland, a vassal of Charlemagne, as Frankish and Moorish soldiers fight in the background.*

Roland's Death in The Song of Roland

The earliest version of The Song of Roland *has been falsely ascribed to Turpin, an archbishop who accompanied Charlemagne on his Spanish campaign. Here is the final scene of this anonymous account, known as* The History of Charlemagne and Roland.

"Roland now blew a loud blast with his horn, to summon any Christian concealed in the adjacent woods to his assistance, or to recall his friends beyond the pass. . . .

The sound reached the king's ears, who lay encamped in the valley still called by his name, about eight miles from Roncevaux, toward Gascony, being carried so far by supernatural power. Charles would have flown to his succor [aid], but was prevented by Ganalon [the traitor] who, conscious of Roland's sufferings, insinuated it was usual with him to sound his horn on light occasions.

'He is perhaps,' said he, 'pursuing some wild beast, and the sound echoes through the woods; it will be fruitless, therefore, to seek him.'

Whilst the soul of the blessed Roland was leaving his body, I Turpin, . . . fell into a trance, and hearing the angelic choir sing aloud, I wondered what it might be. Now, when they had ascended on high, behold there came after them a phalanx of terrible ones, like warriors returning from the spoil bearing their prey. Presently I inquired of one of them what it meant, and was answered,

'We are bearing the soul of Mansir to hell, but yonder is Michael [the angel] bearing the Horn-winder to heaven.'

I told the king what I had seen; and whilst I was yet speaking, behold Baldwin rode up on Roland's horse, and related what had befallen him, and where he had left the hero, in the agonies of earth, beside a stone in the meadows at the foot of the mountain; whereupon the whole army immediately marched back to Roncevaux.

When Charles discovered the corpse of Roland lying in the form of a cross, he began to lament over him with bitter sighs and sobs, wringing his hands and tearing his hair and beard. There did Charles mourn for Roland to the very last day of his life. On the spot where he died he encamped, and caused the body to be embalmed with balsam, myrrh, and aloes. The whole camp watched it that night, honoring his corpse with hymns and songs and innumerable torches and fires kindled on the adjacent mountains."

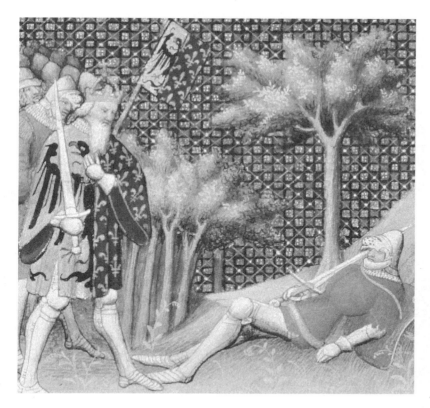

A grief-stricken Charlemagne approaches the body of his vassal Roland. According to the poem The Song of Roland, *Roland blew a horn to summon help, but the traitor Ganalon delayed Charlemagne, who arrived to find Roland dead.*

appear to be embellishments introduced by later storytellers, we know from Einhard's biography that Charles did take a number of his closest advisers with him.

He also traveled with his wife Hildegard and their children—his oldest son, Charles, who was then six, their daughter Rotrude, and a second son, Carloman, who was just over a year old. During the march to Spain, Hildegard gave birth to their third son, Louis.

The plan for the Spanish campaign, which had been formulated the year before at Paderborn, was to join forces with rebel Moors and take the cities of Saragossa and Navarre in northeastern Spain. However, when Charles and his army reached Saragossa, they discovered that their principal Moorish ally, Emir ibn Habib, had been assassinated and his army dissolved. Charles realized that he did not have enough strength to challenge the powerful Moors in their heavily fortified cities.

Tragic Defeat at Roncevaux

While still in Spain, Charles received disturbing news from Saxony. Witikind, the rebel Saxon chieftain, had again taken advantage of Charles's absence and was leading another Saxon revolt. Therefore, without engaging a single Moor in combat or conquering a single Moorish city, Charles decided to leave Spain and return to his more pressing problems in the

The epic hero Roland, shown here amidst attacking Moors, is actually based on Count Hroudland, who died in a skirmish between a small company of Charlemagne's army and the Basques.

north. Upon their return journey through the Pyrenees, a small company of Charles's army, whose duty was to guard the provisions train at the rear of the march, was trapped in a particularly narrow mountain pass, called Roncevaux, and Basque mountaineers massacred the men.

Among those killed by the Basques was Charles's vassal and close personal friend, Count Hroudland, who has lived on in legend as Roland, the perfect knight. The defeat at Roncevaux held little military significance, and yet, according to Einhard, Charles was deeply saddened—perhaps by the loss of several close friends or just because he was not accustomed to defeat.

Whatever the reason, Charles seemed to dwell disproportionately on the loss of his train of provisions at Roncevaux. Einhard describes the situation in some detail:

Dense forests, which stretch in all directions, make this a spot most suitable for setting ambushes. At a moment when Charles' army was stretched out in a long column of march, as the nature of the local [landscape] forced it to be, these Basques, who had set their ambush on the very top of one of the mountains, came rushing down on the last part of the baggage train and the troops who were marching in support of the rear guard and so protecting the army which had gone on ahead. The Basques forced them down into the valley beneath, joined battle with them and killed them to the last man. They then snatched up the baggage, and, protected as they were by the cover of darkness, which was just beginning to fall, scattered in all directions without losing a moment. In this feat the Basques were helped by the lightness of their arms and by the nature of the terrain in which the battle was fought. On the other hand, the heavy nature of their own equipment and the unevenness of the ground completely hampered the Franks in their resistance to the Basques. In this battle died Eggihard, who was in charge of the King's table, Anshelm, the Count of the Palace, and Roland, Lord of the Breton Marches, along with a great number of others. What is more, this assault could not be avenged there and then, for, once it was over, the enemy dispersed in such a way that no one knew where or among which people they could be found.[29]

Why Did the Deeds of Charles and His Paladins Become Legend?

The glorification of Roland in the famous epic poem *The Song of Roland* may be at least partially explained as an effort to find some meaning in the serious losses of the Spanish campaign. However, the endurance of such legends says much about how historians, storytellers, and poets of the Middle Ages glorified and romanticized Charles and his vassals. *The Song of Roland* and other romances about Charlemagne and his legendary knights became the model for later romances about King Arthur and his knights of the round table.

In fact, these stories are the basis for many medieval ideals of what a king is supposed to be and how he is supposed to act. The code of knighthood, or loyalty to one's feudal lord, is also embodied in the legend of Roland, who died the perfect death in defense of his king. In spite of the obvious mythologizing and fictionalizing, the deeds of Charlemagne and his paladins are grounded in fact and deserve their place of honor.

To this day, Charles and his paladins are the basis of popular opinion on how knights and kings ought to behave. The actual Hroudland may not have fought or died as valiantly as the poetic Roland, and surely the actual Battle of Roncevaux was less critical than its poetic counterpart. Nevertheless, the actual Hroudland was probably a great leader who displayed great moral virtue, courage, loyalty, heroism, and intelligence. Charles's paladins were men who inspired confidence and zeal, of which their legends are genuine but distorted testimony.

The source of the legends, too, is genuine, and that source is Charles. This idea was expressed eloquently by G. P. Baker in his 1932 book, *Charles and the United States of Europe:*

> He [Charles] and his servants became the by-word for certain sorts of moral virtue—the qualities of courage, loyalty, heroism, and originality. It was no dull atmosphere of routine that surrounded him. Where he was, there

The deeds of Charlemagne and his paladins became larger-than-life legends and provided a model for later ideals of kings and knights.

were youth and adventure and interest and excitement and gossip and scandal. He was a heartening man. To be near him was to be near the fire.

Charles the Great created more ideas than we realize. The standard knightly conduct was not the only one which he impressed upon Europe. Before his days it was by no means a foregone conclusion that kingship would be a romantic tradition of high idealism and lofty devotion, of respect for law, care for religion and zeal for education. The man who made it this was Charles. He designed and cut out the pattern of the perfect monarch, which was to guide the judgment of mankind at large for a thousand years to come. If we call Louis XIV a bad king, we do so only because he does not square with Charles's pattern. Our standard is one that was set up not by ourselves, but by a king. Why do we demand of a king certain qualities which we do not ask of a bank president or mayor? The answer is, that Charles taught us to look for them. Many vassals had died before Roland—but Charles twisted the thing into high and passionate romance. Many kings had done their duty before Charles himself—but Charles clothed it with an epic splendour. Not only so, but he forced his standard upon us. He made us think as he thought and believe as he believed. The atheist and the republican today test bishops and kings, not by a rule of their own, but by Charles's rule.[30]

5 The Founding of the German Nation

Although the legends about Charlemagne usually tell of his battles with the Saracens, his most important military achievements took place in Saxony and Bavaria, lands which now make up the greater part of Germany. These additions to the Frankish kingdom laid the foundation for the German nation. In fact, Charles's Spanish campaign of 778 turned out to be an ill-advised distraction from the more important task of securing these German lands.

He may be forgiven, though, for failing to anticipate the difficulties that lay ahead in the conquest of Saxony. The ease with which he had swept through Westphalia and Eastphalia one year earlier, when his fast-moving armies caught the Saxons off guard, quite likely led him to underestimate the difficulty of holding on to these lands. In all, more than thirty years of military occupation were required before the Saxons eventually accepted Frankish rule. In addition, the Bavarians never gave up their claim to independence, although they begrudgingly fulfilled their oaths of loyalty to Charles.

As the years of Charles's reign went by, his vision of a unified Christian civilization became clearer. Though he may have been ruthless in battle, he was more generous and fair in victory than most conquerors before or since his time. When victorious in battle, he released most of his prisoners or sent them to monasteries. Instead of keeping all the lands he conquered, he often returned them to their owners in exchange for oaths of feudal loyalty; otherwise, he gave them to the church.

Apparently he had little interest in personal titles or wealth. He believed that the people he conquered, freed from their superstitious religions and their tribal rivalries, would be happier and more prosperous. Once they had experienced life under his rule, he expected his new subjects to forget their old leaders and their old religion quickly. That may be why Charles made the mistake of abandoning Saxony in 777 to undertake his Spanish campaign. In dealing with the Saxons, he greatly overestimated the sincerity of their Christian conversion and greatly underestimated their resistance to foreign dominance.

Saxon Resistance

The Saxon people had accepted their baptisms and sworn their loyalty to Charles under threat of death. Many of them missed their old way of life and resented the new occupants of their homeland.

Charles's Democratic View of Education

De Carolo Magno (Charles the Great) was written by a contemporary of Charlemagne's known only as the Monk of St. Gall. The story of Charles encouraging a group of poor students may not be historically accurate, but it reflects the image of Charles held by his contemporaries.

"After a long absence, Charles returned to Gaul and caused the children, whom he had left with Clement as his pupils, to be brought before him. He required them to be examined, and was amazed at the commendable progress of the poorer class of children, whose written productions were most creditable to them. On the other hand, those of illustrious parentage showed very poor specimens of their skill.

He then set the good scholars on his right, and the poor on his left, saying: 'I praise you much, dear children, for your excellent efforts, . . . and shall ever regard you as persons of merit.'

Then he turned in anger to those on his left . . . as he cried out to them: 'Look here, ye scions of our best nobility, ye pampered ones who, trusting to your birth or fortune, have disobeyed me, and instead of studying, as you were bound, and I expected you to do, have wasted your time in idleness, on play, luxury, or unprofitable occupation. . . . By the king of heaven, let others admire you as much as they please; as for me, I set little store by your birth or beauty; understand ye and remember it well, that unless you give heed speedily to amend your past negligence by diligent study, you will never obtain anything from Charles.' "

When the threat was gone, they went back to their traditional religious practices and ignored Charles's emissaries.

From the Franks' perspective, the Saxons seemed ungrateful and untrustworthy. At least that is how Einhard judged them:

This war could have been brought to a more rapid conclusion, had it not been for the faithlessness of the Saxons. It is hard to say just how many times they were beaten and surrendered as suppliants to Charlemagne, promising to do all that was exacted from them, giving the hostages who were demanded, and this without delay, and receiving the ambassadors who were sent to them. Sometimes they were so cowed and reduced that they even promised to abandon their devil worship and submit willingly to the Christian faith; but, however ready they might seem from time to time to do all this, they were always prepared to break the promises they had made. I cannot really judge which of these two courses can be said to have come the more easily to the Saxons, for, since the very beginning of the war against them, hardly a year passed in which they did not vacillate between surrender and defiance.[31]

The Saxons Invade Frankia

The Saxons learned from their defeat in 777 that they could not overcome the Franks until they overcame their own clan rivalries. Thus, in the spring of 778, while Charles was busy marching to Spain, Witikind, the Saxon chieftain, organized a federation of clan leaders whose armies swept westward, overthrowing all of Charles's fortresses in Saxony. Except for the highest ranking officers, the Saxon armies marched on foot. When they reached the borders of Saxony, they marched fifty or sixty miles into Austrasia, not stopping until they reached the Rhine River.

Witikind's armies burned the Franks' houses, churches, grain fields, and everything else that was flammable. The Saxons slaughtered Frankish men, women, and children who happened to be in the army's path. When Charles finally received word of Witikind's brutality, he realized that he had to halt his expensive, ill-timed Spanish campaign and return to Saxony.

Relying on the speed of his cavalries, Charles surprised the cumbersome Saxon army of footsoldiers as it was returning from its bloody foray into Austrasia. The Franks killed a great number of the Saxons, but many others, to Charles's dismay, fled. Among these who escaped was Witikind, who once again sought refuge among the Danes in the north.

Charles Marches to the Elbe River

With Witikind momentarily out of the way, Charles found little resistance to his armies as he marched through Westphalia

Frankish soldiers, like this one, were responsible for conquering the rebellious tribes in Saxony and Bavaria, which are now part of modern Germany.

What's in an Oath?

Charles demanded that every freeman in his kingdom swear an oath of fidelity to him. In the following capitula *from Brian Tierney's* Sources of Medieval History, *Charles explains just what this oath meant.*

"Charles commanded that every man in his whole kingdom, whether ecclesiastic or layman . . . down to those who were twelve years old, should now promise their fidelity to him, . . . that all may know this oath contains this meaning:

1. First, that each one voluntarily shall strive, in accordance with his knowledge and ability, to live wholly in the holy service of God. . . .

2. Secondly, that no man, either through perjury or any other fraud, for the flattery or gift of any one, shall refuse to return or dare to conceal a serf of the lord king or a district or land or anything that belongs to him. . . .

3. That no one shall presume to rob or do any injury to the churches of God or widows or orphans or pilgrims; for the lord emperor himself, after God and his saints, has declared himself their protector and defender.

4. That no one shall dare to lay waste a fief of the lord king or make it his own property.

5. That no one shall neglect a summons to war from the lord king; and that no count shall dare to dismiss any of those who owe military service. . . .

6. That no one shall obstruct at all in any way a ban or command of the lord king, or to dally with his work or to impede in any way his will or commands. And that no one shall dare to neglect to pay his dues or taxes.

7. That no one, for any reason, shall make a practice in court of defending another unjustly either from any desire of gain or by obstructing a just judgment by his skill in reasoning, or by a desire to oppress another. That every case shall be tried in accordance with justice and the law; and that no one shall have the power to obstruct justice by a gift, reward, or any kind of evil flattery."

and Eastphalia in the spring of 779. When he ordered a general conference of Eastphalian nobles, the Eastphalians assembled in large numbers, and, once again, many of them accepted baptism. Pleased with the effectiveness of his occupation, Charles led his army farther east, deeper into Germany. At the Elbe River, he stopped and built a semipermanent camp. This was the first time in nearly eight hundred years that a foreign army had invaded so far into Germany. From his camps on the Elbe, Charles experienced his first encounters with the Slav tribes of eastern Europe, but for now he was content to observe them without speaking of yet another conquest.

In the nine years since his first campaign in Saxony, Charles had taken an extraordinary amount of land. He had also learned that taking it and keeping it were two very different matters. Even though most members of the Saxon nobility had sworn their loyalty to him, he knew that he could not yet count on it. And without it, he knew that his military conquests were meaningless.

His kingdom had already grown too large for him to control single-handedly. Charles attempted to continue the tradition of the Frankish king, which was to travel from one royal domain to another throughout his kingdom, but the kingdom had grown too large. Besides occupying Saxony, Charles had solidified his hold on Aquitaine and Italy, and he was continually marching back and forth, trying to cover all his lands.

In the fall of 780, Charles decided to make another trip to Rome with his entire royal court. The royal family reached Pavia, the Lombard capital, before Christmas and spent the winter there. By this time, Charles's family included four sons—Pepin, Charles, Carloman, and Louis—and three daughters—Rotrude, Bertha, and Gisela. All but Pepin, the oldest of the children, had been born to Hildegard. She had given birth to the two youngest sons, Carloman and Louis, during foreign campaigns. Charles's energetic personality and physical stamina were ideally suited for this ambitious lifestyle, and he obviously enjoyed having Hildegard with him. The strain of this unsettled life, however, of giving birth to children and looking after them while traveling across the kingdom weighed more heavily on Hildegard. Although only twenty-five or twenty-six years old, her health was beginning to decline.

Two Young Kings

Nevertheless, Easter Sunday in 781 must have been an especially gratifying day for her, as she observed the special ceremony conducted in Rome for her two youngest sons, Carloman, age four, and Louis, age three. First, both boys were publicly baptized by Pope Hadrian, and then he anointed them and crowned them both as kings. Carloman's name was changed to the more highly revered Pepin, and he was crowned king of Italy. His baby brother, Louis, was crowned king of Aquitaine.

These ceremonial events were not just for show. First, the fact that Carloman's name was changed to Pepin had serious implications for Charles's oldest son, also named Pepin, who was the son of Charles's first wife, Himiltrude. Renaming Carloman suggests that the elder Pepin had been disinherited. This may explain

But what advantage did Charles see in crowning his two toddling sons as kings of Italy and Aquitaine? Obviously, they were too young to rule, but Charles wanted the people to begin thinking of them as kings and to gradually grow accustomed to hearing the phrases King Pepin of Italy and King Louis of Aquitaine. In fifteen years or so, when Pepin and Louis were ready to rule, the people would be ready to accept them. Also, it was not too soon for Charles's sons to begin thinking of themselves as kings and preparing for the day when they would actually rule. In the meantime, of course, Charles was still the man in charge. He had effectively invented another level of feudal command to place between himself and the dukes of both regions. Even when they were old enough to rule for themselves, Pepin and Louis would remain subkings and owe both loyalty and taxes to the king of the Franks.

This tenth-century drawing depicts Charles (left) with his son Pepin (right). In order to prepare his two young sons to rule his large kingdom, Charles made Carloman, renamed Pepin, king of Italy, and Louis was crowned king of Aquitaine.

why, a few years later, the elder Pepin was arrested for conspiring with a group of Bavarian noblemen to overthrow Charles.

The reasons for his disinheritance are vague, but we do know that his mother's marriage to Charles was not recognized by his contemporaries as an official marriage. Einhard mentions the older Pepin only once in his biography of Charlemagne, saying he was "born to Charlemagne by a concubine. He was handsome enough, but a hunchback."[32] In the annals of the Frankish kings, the older Pepin is often called Pepin the Hunchback.

Subkings

Charlemagne may have been a great conqueror, but he was an even greater statesman. In fact, his contributions to the political organization of Europe and to its educational and cultural foundation were far more lasting than his military conquests. Even his military success came more from his organizational genius than from bravery or physical strength. During his entire reign, Charles was occupied with the problem of organizing a new kind of government, one which could stand up to the strongest foreign threats, but which still allowed local rulers to retain a good deal of loyalty and authority among their people.

The Moral Tale of Tancho the Bell Maker

According to the Monk of St. Gall, "God kept watch for the devout King Charlemagne, when his own attention was turned elsewhere by the affairs of the kingdom." One example of such divine intervention occurs in the monk's story of Tancho the Bell Maker.

"There was a craftsman whose skill at moulding bronze and glass was greater than that of anyone else in the world. His name was Tancho and he had formerly been a monk at Saint Gall. He cast a superb bell, and the Emperor was delighted with its tone. This outstanding worker, who was doomed all the same to a terrible fate, said to the Emperor: 'My Imperial master, order a great mass of copper to be delivered to me and I will refine it. Then, instead of tin, give me as much silver as I need, a hundred pounds at least. I will cast you such a bell that this one will seem dumb in comparison.' Charlemagne, who was the most generous of monarchs . . . made no difficulty about ordering everything for which he had asked to be given to him. The rascally monk took delivery of the materials and left in great glee. He smelted and refined the bronze. Instead of the silver, he used the purest tin and soon cast a bell much better than that made of adulterated metal, of which Charlemagne had nevertheless thought so highly. When he had tested the new bell, he presented it to the Emperor. Charlemagne admired the new bell very much for its exquisite shape. He ordered an iron clapper to be fixed inside and then had the bell hung in the bell-tower. This was soon done. The churchwarden, the other attendants in the church, and even a number of boys who were hanging about, all strove, one after the other, to make the bell ring. None of them succeeded. In the end, the monk who had cast the bell and perpetrated this outrageous fraud came over in a rage, seized hold of the rope, and tugged at the bell. The mass of metal slipped from the center of its beam and fell down on the rogue's head. It passed straight through his dead carcass and crashed to the ground. . . . When the mass of silver of which I have told you was discovered, Charlemagne in his justice ordered it to be distributed among the poor of his palace."

As subkings, Charles's two sons represented a new class of noblemen who answered directly to a higher king, yet who were respected and obeyed as kings in their own lands. To local people living in such a large kingdom, the subking was a more tangible ruler than a distant king who lived somewhere on the other side of the mountains. Yet by paying tribute to this local royalty, the people were still acknowledging the authority of the Frankish kings over their local dukes.

Young Charles: The Heir Apparent

With his two younger brothers crowned as kings and the older Pepin disinherited, what was to become of young Charles, the oldest son of Hildegard? Young Charles, who would have been eight or nine at this time, was to remain constantly by his father's side, so that one day he could inherit his father's crown and become the next king of the Franks.

Charlemagne, as noted by his biographers and his contemporary scribes, had extraordinarily strong ties with almost all of his children. During the winter months between military campaigns, the king romped and played with his children or watched their progress under the tutorship of Einhard and a scholar named Alcuin. When the boys were old enough, he took them on expeditions to teach them the arts of the hunter. For in this arena, Charles knew no equals.

Charles's relationship with his namesake was particularly close. Young Charles rode by his father's side as they marched to Saxony, and as the king presided over his general assemblies, young Charles customarily sat to his right. When the time came for young Charles to lead armies by himself, he became his father's best general.

The Massacre at Verden

Most of Charles's victories actually came with little fighting. Through careful planning and organizing, he managed to appear with armies so intimidating that the enemy often surrendered before risking serious losses. Considering the violent nature of warfare in the Middle Ages, Charles's record for avoiding unnecessary violence is remarkable. Still, he was a man of his age, and several brutal encounters with the Saxons have somewhat tarnished his record as a peacemaker. One event, which demonstrates both his zealous hatred of the ancient Germanic religions and his growing impatience with the Saxon rebellions, occurred at a place called Verden in 782.

That spring, Charles had once again called an assembly at Paderborn to assess the progress of his occupation of Saxony. But even as more Saxon noblemen swore their loyalty to Charles, the rebel Witikind struck Charles's camps in eastern and northern Saxony. Charles sent an army, led by Count Theuderic, to attack the rebel Saxons. It was one of the few times when his forces were inadequate. The Saxons routed Theuderic's army at Verden, killing more than twenty of Charles's noblemen. To this day, the hill on which the battle took place is known as Dachtelfeld, or Slap-in-the-Face Hill.

The Saxons' triumph was short-lived, however, as Charles led the rest of his army to Verden. When they arrived, all was quiet. After restoring peace, Charles demanded that the leaders of the Saxon victory surrender. Once again, the crafty Witikind and the other rebel leaders had mysteriously disappeared. In their place, Charles rounded up forty-five hundred Saxons, including women and children, and gave orders to have them all beheaded.

These innocent victims suffered for the antagonism, frustration, and humiliation that their leaders had inflicted on Charles. Verden was not the first time that the leaders of the Saxon rebellion had struck a serious blow to Charles's ambitions. For a dozen frustrating years, Witikind had antagonized Charles and then escaped his grasp. Based upon past experience, Witikind assumed that Charles was bluffing and would not harm these innocent civilians.

Charles, however, was fed up. He gave the rebel leaders the choice of coming forth to either fight or surrender to gain the release of their countrymen. When Witikind did neither, he forced Charles's hand. The horrible slaughter of forty-five hundred innocent people seems so out of character for Charles, but many historians have used this incident to judge Charles's moral character. In the end the Verden massacre apparently achieved its purpose, which was to deter more Saxons from joining Witikind's revolt.

The Deaths of Hildegard and Bertrada

The massacre at Verden occurred in September 782, one of the few times that Charles's wife Hildegard was not with him. She was pregnant again, and this time she was just too weak to remain in camp, so she had departed for home. When Charles returned from Saxony to his domain in Heristal that winter, Hildegard was too sick and too weak to be moved. They spent the winter in Heristal, awaiting the birth of their seventh child. On April 30, 783, Hildegard died after giving birth to a daughter. The baby girl was named after her mother, but she, too, was too weak to survive.

Charles's private life, which had been so rich and peaceful during his marriage to Hildegard, now grew less so. Less than three months after Hildegard's death, his mother also died. Charles and his mother had always been close. She had lived at the royal court and was always a source of warmth and support for her son. Einhard tells us:

> His mother, Bertrada, had lived with him to old age in great honour. He treated her with the utmost reverence, so that no quarrel of any kind ever arose between them—except in the matter of the divorce of the daughter of King Desiderius, whom he had married at her bidding. Bertrada . . . lived to see three grandsons and as many granddaughters in her son's house. Charles had his mother buried with great honour in the same great St. Denys Church in which his father lay.[33]

Charles remarried several months later, taking for his queen Fastrada, the daughter of a Frankish count, Radolf. Although this marriage produced two more daughters, it was not destined to be a very happy period in Charles's life. For one thing, during his ten-year marriage to Fastrada, he was distracted by two conspiracies to overthrow him, one of which was orchestrated by his first son, Pepin the Hunchback.

Capitularies Concerning Saxony

The massacre at Verden also demonstrates a hardening of Charles's resolve to subdue the Saxons and stamp out their pagan rituals. He followed up the massacre with a new set of ordinances called *Capitularies Concerning Saxony* in 784. These ordinances authorized severe new punishments against any Saxons who resisted the Franks or practiced the old Saxon religion:

> Whoever enters a church by violence, or forcibly removes or steals any object from it, or sets fire to the building, shall be put to death.

> Whoever refuses to respect the Lenten fast out of contempt for Christianity and eats meat during the season, shall be put to death.

> Whoever kills a bishop, a priest, or a deacon, shall be put to death.

> Whoever burns the body of a dead person according to pagan ritual and reduces the bones to ash shall be put to death.

> Any unbaptized Saxon who seeks to hide among his compatriots and refuses to request the sacrament, shall be put to death.

> Whoever fails to abide by the fidelity owed to the king, shall be put to death.[34]

The tough new policy brought even more suffering to the Saxons than the massacre at Verden. Virtually any Saxon taken prisoner could be executed on grounds of one or more of the terror capitularies, as they came to be called. Wherever the Frankish armies went, they set fire to fields and villages. During the spring of 784, unusually heavy rains fell on the bare, scorched ground washing the soil into the rivers and streams, which became swollen and flooded.

Hundreds of thousands of Saxons died of starvation that summer, and when winter came, instead of heading home and giving the Saxons a reprieve as he did most winters, Charles decided to stay and keep the pressure on. When it finally became too cold and wet even for the Franks to remain on the march, Charles set up camps for his army around his palace at Eresburg. From there, Frankish raiding parties continued to terrorize the countryside.

Witikind Surrenders

When spring came, Charles pursued Witikind farther north than he had ever ventured before. Witikind, still the heart and soul of Saxon resistance, managed to outrun Charles's army, but everywhere the Franks went they completely devastated the land and villages. Finally, a group of Saxon messengers carried an offer of peace from Charles to Witikind, on the condition of Witikind's surrender.

Seeing the futility of his position and the suffering of his people, Witikind finally agreed to Charles's terms. As usual, they were generous. Witikind came to Charles's villa at Attigny in Austrasia where he swore his lifelong allegiance to the Frankish king and received baptism. In these last two years of the Saxon wars, Charles had taken a harder, more ruthless stand against the Saxon people, and he finally achieved peace in Saxony.

After years of bitter fighting between the Saxons and the Franks, Saxon chieftain Witikind surrenders to Charlemagne in 785.

Charles Subdues the Duke of Bavaria

With his conquest of Saxony complete, Charles turned his attention to Bavaria, the great alpine region south of Saxony, in what is now southeastern Germany. Unlike the Saxons, most Bavarians had already given up their pagan ways for Christianity, and the Bavarian nobility had officially been vassals of the Frankish monarchy since the time of the Merovingian kings. However, the Bavarians were somewhat isolated by the Bavarian Alps from the heartland of the Frankish kingdom, which lay east of the Rhine River. Therefore, the Bavarians had grown accustomed to their independence.

Their duke, Tassilo, had allied himself through marriage with the old Lombard royal family of Desiderius. Although Charles had settled his own quarrels with the Lombards long ago, Desiderius had

Charlemagne watches with satisfaction as a subdued Witikind is baptized.
Charlemagne usually allowed his conquered subjects to keep their authority
over their own people, as long as they accepted Christianity and swore
allegiance to him.

made no secret of his resentment of Charles, and it seems to have rubbed off on Tassilo. He refused to attend Charles's assemblies or send representatives from his court, and he had ignored his feudal obligation to help Charles during the Saxon wars.

For all of these transgressions, Charles decided that Tassilo must be taught a lesson and that Bavaria must be tied more tightly to the Frankish realm. To accomplish this, Charles organized the most formidable military alliance he had ever put together. In 787 an Italian army, carrying before them their ten-year-old king,

Pepin, approached Bavaria from the south. At the same time, a Saxon army marched into Bavaria from the north, and Charles led a Frankish army from the east. The assembled forces so overwhelmed any possible resistance from the Bavarians that no major battles were even necessary.

Tassilo sized up the situation quickly. Charles's army was camped near the city of Augsberg, where Tassilo appeared before him. In an elaborate ceremony, Tassilo surrendered the duchy of Bavaria. Humbly apologizing for his disobedience, he presented to Charles a small staff with the figure of a man engraved on it. Symbolically, he was handing over his duchy, as an ordinary fief, to his lord to whom he had been disloyal. Charles took the staff momentarily; then he handed it right back to Tassilo, reconfirming that Tassilo was his vassal. In addition, Charles gave Tassilo a gold bracelet and a horse covered with a gold-cloth blanket. An anonymous eyewitness tells us that Charles, while presenting these gifts, said, "Receive, my son, these symbols of your vassalage." Tassilo reportedly kneeled and kissed the king's knees, responding, "Oh king, you wield your office for the happiness of the world, and I acknowledge my service to you, world without end."[35]

It may seem strange that after mustering such an enormous army to force Tassilo's surrender, Charles turned right around and returned his title and his duchy. But the great show of force had accomplished its purpose, and this ceremony was an important symbolic act confirming it. In those days when most people, even among the nobility, could not read or write, no written treaty would be recalled as vividly as the memory of Tassilo kneeling humbly before the king of the Franks and kissing the king's knees. All those in attendance would surely recall how Tassilo had publicly and unmistakably placed Bavaria under the rule of the Frankish king.

The Mystery of Tassilo's Treason

Also, by restoring the title of duke to Tassilo, Charles followed the same federalist principles he had established in Lombardia, Aquitaine, Italy, and Saxony. As long as the rulers swore their loyalty to him,

Charles stood back and let them rule their lands as they saw fit. In the spring of 788, however, something made Charles change his mind about Tassilo.

Exactly what happened is enshrouded in the mystery of inaccurate records, and, perhaps, secretive intentions. By the accounts of most Frankish annalists, Tassilo's wife Liutberga was to blame. As the daughter of Desiderius, she had good reason to resent Charles. He had rejected her sister, Desiderata, defeated her father, and humiliated her husband.

That spring, a year after Tassilo's surrender, Charles called for a general assembly at Ingilenheim, on the Main River in Austrasia. This time, Tassilo attended the assembly, suggesting that he had learned his lesson and that he had no reason to fear for his own safety. It must have come as quite a surprise to everyone in attendance, then, when some of Tassilo's own men rose at the convention to accuse him of conspiring against Charles with the heathen Avars, whose lands lay just east of Bavaria.

That Tassilo, who had so recently sworn his allegiance to this powerful king, would now conspire against him with these much despised, barbaric warriors, was a shocking charge, hardly to be believed. In fact, no one can say with certainty whether it was true, or whether the accusation was simply a trumped-up charge that enabled Charles to dispose of Tassilo once and for all. We do know that Tassilo was immediately taken prisoner, tried, and convicted of treason. The duchy of Bavaria was divided into counties, which were awarded to loyal noblemen, some Frankish and some Bavarian, but all solid vassals of Charles. Tassilo was sentenced to death, but Charles commuted the sentence to life in a monastery.

Charles, shown here in his tent while on a military campaign, confronted the insubordinate Tassilo, duke of Bavaria, with a powerful army.

Charles Defends Bavaria

More importantly, Charles now had a new enemy, the Avars, or Huns, who invaded Bavaria shortly after Tassilo's trial. We do not know if they were expecting Tassilo's armies to help protect them and guide them through Bavaria on the roads to the Frankish kingdom, or if the Huns knew of Tassilo's fall and had come to exploit the Bavarians at a weak moment. What they found instead was Charles's army waiting for them, and they suffered a great slaughter. Many of the Avars tried to flee and were drowned in the Danube.

Charles's quick and decisive defense of Bavaria won the support of most Bavarian noblemen. Consequently, Charles was able to break up the old duchy and establish smaller counties in its place. These drastic changes would have met far greater resistance from the Bavarians had they not been convinced of Tassilo's treachery and Charles's willingness to protect them from the Avars.

By the end of 788, Charles's conquests in what is now Germany were complete. Although future campaigns in these regions would continue to put down minor rebellions, neither the Saxons nor the Bavarians now posed a serious threat to his rule. Although Charles's huge kingdom was destined to break into pieces at the hands of land-hungry noblemen, two great nations, France and Germany, would eventually emerge from this kingdom. While these two nations reflect the linguistic differences of the tribes that settled them during the period of the Great Migration, they also share a powerful bond of political order, church influence, and the cultural and educational heritage passed down through their nobility from the time of Charlemagne.

Chapter

6 A Prosperous Kingdom

Charles's greatest military efforts in the years after 788 were aimed at conquering Pannonia, which is that part of Europe now occupied by Slovakia, the Czech Republic, and Hungary. This task was, in many ways, more daunting than the conquest of Saxony. The targeted lands lay four hundred miles from Austrasia, and they were occupied by a tribe of people known as the Avars, or Huns, whose warriors were accomplished horsemen like the Franks.

War with the Avars

Fortunately, Charles was at the height of his power and prestige, and in 794, he was able to assemble his largest army ever and march across the Danube River into Pannonia. Though no written records of the actual conflict have survived, Einhard mentions that the Franks' victory was so thorough that afterward the Avars completely abandoned Pannonia:

> Just how many battles were fought and how much blood was shed is shown by the fact that Pannonia is now completely uninhabited and that the site of the Khan's palace is now so deserted that no evidence remains that

anyone ever lived there. All the Hun nobility died in this war, all their glory departed. All their wealth and their treasures assembled over so many years were dispersed.[36]

The greatest victory of the war against the Avars was won by Charles's son Pepin, king of Italy, whose army conquered the Avars' mighty citadel, known as the Ring because it was surrounded and protected by nine concentric walls. In this fortress the Avars stored vast treasures of gold, silver, and precious gems that they had collected during more than two hundred years of conquest in eastern Europe and central Asia. Pepin now loaded all this treasure on wagons and hauled it to his father's palace at Aachen.

For all their advances in civilization, the Franks had never been known for possessing great treasures or riches. Therefore, according to Einhard, when Pepin's men unloaded the Avar treasures at Charles's feet, the Franks were astounded:

> The memory of man cannot recall any war against the Franks by which they were so enriched and their material possessions so increased. These Franks, who until then had seemed almost paupers, now discovered so much gold and silver in the palace and captured

Charles addresses his nobles. The Frankish kingdom was not known for its wealth, but the capture of the Ring, or the Avar fortress, brought vast treasures to the Franks.

so much precious booty in their battles, that it could rightly be maintained that they had in all justice taken from the Huns what these last had unjustly stolen from other nations.[37]

Charles Abandons the Conquest of Hungary

Contrary to Einhard's account, Pepin's army did not kill all of the Avar nobility. Some noblemen, in fact, accompanied Pepin to Aachen, where they were baptized and swore their allegiance to Charles.

In 795, the year the Franks captured the Ring, Charles was fifty-one years old, which was quite old for those days. He probably realized how futile it would be to

continue the war against these tribes, so he discontinued his campaigns into this region. The greatest benefits of the Avaric wars were indirect. They greatly reduced the threat of an eastern invasion of Bavaria, while they increased the loyalty of the Bavarians.

Charles did not try to Christianize and civilize the native population of Pannonia as he had the Saxons. He simply held this region as a protectorate to help buffer Bavaria and Saxony from the tribes of eastern Europe. If Charles had learned one key lesson in all of his conquests, it was that he could not afford to ignore Saxony. This vast region of northern Germany on Frankia's eastern border was the most important of all Charles's conquests and the one he had worked hardest to Christianize and civilize. Following his conquest of the Ring, therefore, Charles withdrew most of his Frankish, Italian, and Saxon vassals from Pannonia and sent them on another expedition to Saxony. This time he was interested in the northernmost region of Saxony, known as Wihmodia.

Charles had ignored Wihmodia in the past because this flat peninsula on the North Sea with its marshes and rivers was not easy for mounted cavalries to cross. Most of the rich marshland had been reclaimed from the mouths of numerous rivers that emptied into the sea. Over hundreds of years, the Saxons had built dams and dikes to drain the water from the land and direct it into canals and reservoirs. An army on horseback was slow to cross a land covered with such barriers.

Nevertheless, Charles had been planning a march on Wihmodia for some time, and he ordered engineers and carpenters to build a train of floating pontoons that could be broken down into

The Legendary Size of the Avars' Ring

The Monk of St. Gall's biography of Charles includes this fanciful description of the Ring, or the citadel of the Avars. It is presented in the form of a dialogue that the monk claims he had as a boy with an old soldier named Adalbert.

"'The country of the Huns was surrounded with nine rings—'

'Rings?' asked the boy.

'It was protected by nine walls, or palisades,' explained the old soldier. 'The diameter of the first ring [that is, the space enclosed between the first and second rings] was equal to the distance from Zurich to Constance.

'The palisades were constructed of oak, beech, and pine logs, twenty feet in height and twenty feet in width, filled in with stones and lime, and closely covered above with sod. Trees were planted on the edges. Within the enclosures the farms and villages were so disposed as to distance that each was so near the other as to fall within reach of the voice. The impregnable walls had narrow gates through which those living within or without the immediate enclosure were wont to issue forth on their predatory excursions. The distance from the second ring, which resembled the first in construction, to the third was equal to twenty German or forty Italian miles, and so on to the ninth, although each succeeding ring was much wider than that before. Homesteads, moreover, were so distributed between the rings, that trumpet-signals given in one were easily heard in the other.'"

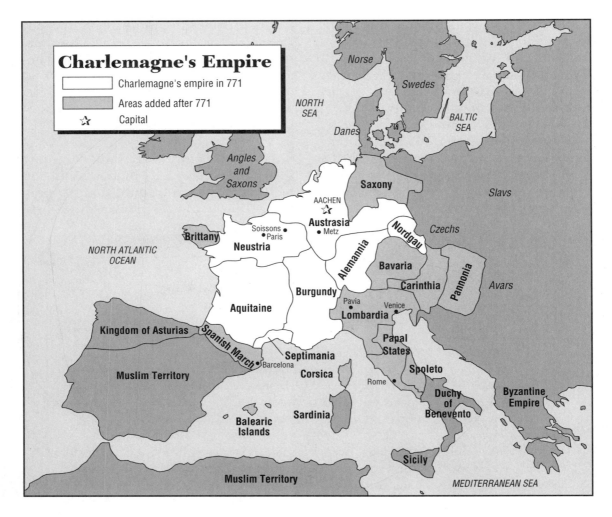

Charlemagne's Empire

- ☐ Charlemagne's empire in 771
- ▨ Areas added after 771
- ☆ Capital

NORTH SEA

NORTH ATLANTIC OCEAN

Norse

Swedes

BALTIC SEA

Danes

Angles and Saxons

Saxony

Slavs

AACHEN ☆

Austrasia
Metz

Nordgau

Czechs

Brittany

Soissons
Paris

Neustria

Alemannia

Bavaria

Pannonia

Avars

Carinthia

Burgundy

Aquitaine

Lombardia
Pavia

Venice

Kingdom of Asturias

Spanish March

Barcelona

Septimania

Corsica

Papal States

Rome

Spoleto

Byzantine Empire

Muslim Territory

Balearic Islands

Sardinia

Duchy of Benevento

Sicily

Muslim Territory

MEDITERRANEAN SEA

four pieces and reassembled wherever they were needed. Traveling alternately by pontoon and on foot, the Frankish army forced its way over the dikes, floated across the reservoirs, and stormed the Saxon earthworks of Wihmodia one inch at a time. Finally, in September of 797, Charles and his vassals stood on the shores of Hadeln and looked out upon the North Sea. They had carried out a conquest first envisioned eight centuries earlier by Julius Caesar, the first Roman emperor.

The Saxon Deportation Policy

After thirty years of war, Charles had also learned something about handling the conquered Saxons. He had tried being lenient and allowing the Saxons to continue their traditional ways, only to have to face one rebellion after another. In 784 he had gone to the other extreme, implementing *Capitularies Concerning Saxony* and executing thousands of people for the crime of practicing their traditional customs. In Wihmodia, he hit upon a happy medium: deportation. One-third of the Saxon families in the conquered region were rounded up and removed from their land. Charles had them transported to other areas of the Frankish kingdom. Those who remained behind were required to take an oath of fealty and accept baptism. In this way, Charles was able to break up the traditional tribal associations without bloodshed.

Thus, by the time the last Saxon stronghold was overthrown in 797, Charles was able to relax his repression of the Saxon people. That winter, he invited Frankish and Saxon lords to a council at Aachen to revise the *Capitularies Concerning Saxony*. He removed the death penalty for carrying out harmless non-Christian traditions. Most importantly, in the original Saxon capitularies the Franks had been declared superiors over all Saxons, but the new capitularies considered the two peoples as equals. The new Saxon capitularies of 797 reflect Charles's belief that the Franks and Saxons could now live together in harmony and equality. Of course, just like every Frankish landholder, all Saxon landholders were required to swear an oath of fealty to him.

Contributions of the Subkings, Pepin and Louis

The stability of Charles's kingdom was also aided now by the strong leadership of his sons, Pepin and Louis. The plan that Charles had put into place in 781, making Pepin and Louis kings of Italy and Aquitaine, respectively, was now beginning to pay off. While Pepin had conquered the Avars, Louis expanded the Frankish kingdom into northern Spain, where the Franks had never before been able to penetrate. With the able military assistance of William of Toulouse, Louis conquered Spanish cities as far down the Mediterranean coast as Barcelona.

The Organization of Charles's Government

With leadership and stability provided by his sons and chief vassals, Charles could now review the organization of his government and the quality of domestic life within his kingdom. In the thirty years that he had been king, his government had evolved from a weak federation of independent noblemen to a relatively strong network of emissaries and representatives carrying out the rulings of his central command.

The most dominant characteristic of government in Charles's time was, of course, the system of military aristocracy that blended Germanic and Roman traditions of a soldier's loyalty to his general. When Charles first became king, these traditions had already produced a pattern of strong, independent local rule among the counts and viscounts. To them the king was still primarily a military leader with limited administrative powers. His kingdom was too large, and his administrators too few and inefficient to carry his authority effectively to all his subjects.

Charles divided his kingdom among approximately three hundred counts. A small number of counts held the title of *marchio*, or ruler of a march. The term *march* was given to frontier territories that

Charlemagne receives gifts from his subjects in the Spanish March. Charlemagne held ultimate control over the entire kingdom, but he appointed loyal vassals to govern the various territories, marches, and counties under Frankish rule.

had been gained by military conquest, such as the Spanish March, the March of Brittany, and the March of Friuli. The modern title of marquis is derived from this term.

Somewhat more independence was conceded to approximately ten dukes, who presided over the formerly independent kingdoms of Britanny, Burgundy, Alemannia, Bavaria, Aquitaine, Gascony, Provence, Lombardia, Benevento, and Spoleto. As these lands became increasingly controlled by the Franks and the Roman Church, the title of duke was typically given to one of Charles's Frankish vassals. By 795, all of these dukes had been forced to swear allegiance to Charles or one of his sons. Those who failed to prove their loyalty, like Tassilo of Bavaria, were relieved of their titles and sent to live in a monk's cell.

Charles Strengthens His Administration

When Charles first took the throne, the closest thing that he had to an administration was a group of clergy called the chapel, whose job was to supervise the writing of royal correspondence, treaties, and other royal documents. Charles's court consisted of a steward, a butler, a chamberlain, and a constable. Supervising these officials was the count of the palace, who no doubt considered himself superior to the rest. Yet neither he nor any members of the court had any authority over dukes, counts, and local lords.

Charles did everything in his power to eliminate these serious limitations of his royal authority. First, he took advantage of his military authority to keep his noblemen busy. In May of almost every year since he had become king, Charles had called a general assembly to launch a military campaign, usually into Saxony. He skillfully used these assemblies to link economic and judicial business with the military business at hand.

Charles used the written word to strengthen his own hand. Charles ordered the clerics of his chapel to record his rulings, especially those made at the general assemblies. These rulings were the first collections of written law to develop in Europe since the fall of the Romans. That is one reason Charles placed such great emphasis on education and literacy in his court. Rulings that were preserved in writing were far more exact, and therefore carried greater weight, than the local customs and punishments that were passed on by word of mouth.

The Capitularies

A capitulary was a collection of rulings, or *capitula*. Although they were written, which was a significant step forward in the Frankish judicial system, they could hardly be described as a systematic or uniform code of law. During his reign, Charles was responsible for at least 113 capitularies, containing more than eleven hundred *capitula*, that regulated weights, measures, road tolls, currencies, trade regulations,

A charter signed by Charlemagne. The Frankish king ordered his rulings to be written down to ensure that they would be clear and obeyed. These capitularies were the first collections of written law in Europe since the fall of the Romans.

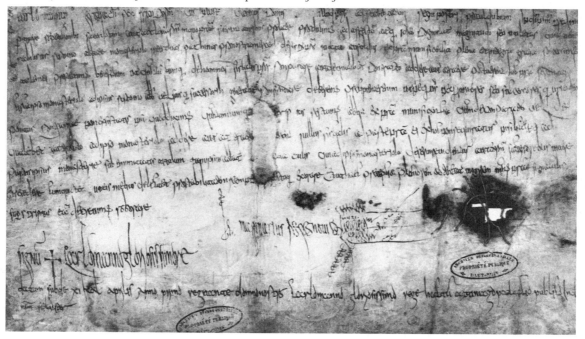

military service, and religious practices and stipulated penalties for pickpocketing, stealing, assault, rape, and murder.

The general assemblies wrote most of the capitularies. Not so coincidentally, virtually every capitulary begins with a declaration that "all with one consent assented thereto." In other words, they were approved unanimously. That is hardly remarkable when one considers that Charles had the power to repeal titles and revoke lands from anyone he considered disloyal.

Many of Charles's rulings concerning government business, such as road tolls (pictured), commerce regulation, and law enforcement, were recorded in capitularies, or written collections of laws.

Missi Dominici, or Emissaries of the King

To see that his orders were followed, Charles relied on his handpicked *missi dominici*, or "emissaries of the king." Although this diplomatic corps was not Charles's invention, he elevated its stature to new levels. His father and grandfather also had *missi*, but both Charles Martel and Pepin chose their messengers from among the poorer, lower ranking vassals in the kingdom. The *missi* were essentially messengers who carried the kings' rulings, calls to assembly, or demands for war supplies to the far corners of the kingdom. Charles, however, selected his *missi* from his most powerful and influential vassals—the highest ranking and most loyal of his counts, bishops, and abbots. As they traveled throughout the kingdom, Charles's *missi* not only relayed his messages and heard complaints from noblemen but also were empowered to secure an oath of fealty from every freeman in the kingdom.

The *missi* also had the power to judge and enforce the compliance with the capitularies. For this purpose they held their own court sessions and appointed knights and clerics to positions as jurists, or *scapini*. The *missi dominici* of Charles's reign reinforced the idea of one king ruling over all his subjects, including his counts and dukes.

A Rise in Commerce

As time went on, the royal government grew in size and influence. The rise in bureaucracy triggered a chain reaction of social changes. More roads were built to accommodate the increase in travel throughout the kingdom and the protectorates of Frankia, and the increase in roads produced even more trade and commerce across the kingdom. Responsibility for maintaining these roads fell to the local lords, who owned the land on which the roads lay. Most noblemen turned this burden into an opportunity to charge tolls to all those travelers who crossed their land. These noblemen and the growing class of merchants also relied more and more on exchanging coins than on directly bartering for goods. The new system of commerce required educated clerks who could read and do arithmetic.

Education Under Charles the Great

In the courts and marketplaces throughout his kingdom, then, Charles saw a growing demand for education. In the fall of 781, a group of church scholars from the famous English monastery at York visited Charles. He was most impressed by an older scholar named Alcuin, who was invited to remain in court and help Charles organize the schools of his empire. Alcuin was one of the most remarkable scholars of his or any other age. His letters to Charles were the source of much of the wisdom of the capitularies. Charles's lofty aim of building a Christian empire can also be traced to the influence of Alcuin, as can the more merciful treatment of enemies that Charles showed in his later campaigns.

Perhaps Alcuin's most famous contribution to Charles's court was his work as

Charles, shown here dictating, increased travel and trade in Frankia, prompting the building and maintaining of roads and the use of coins for exchange instead of goods or services.

director of the palace school. The primary duty of this school, which had been a part of the royal court at least since the time of Charles Martel, was to educate the king's children and the children of members of the royal court. Alcuin, however, also conducted a school for the most prominent members of the court, including Einhard; the abbot Adalhard; the archbishops of Mayence, Salzburg, and Orleans; and, of course, Charles himself.

Charlemagne visits a school. The king of the Franks had a particular affinity for education, and he studied Greek and Latin literature, astronomy, science, and theology with other members of his court.

These illustrious officials met at Charles's court to discuss theology, classical Greek and Latin literature, science, and astrology. At Alcuin's bidding, they all dropped their true names and assumed the names of biblical and mythical heroes. Charles, for example, was called David, the greatest of the biblical kings of Jerusalem. One of the bishops was called Homer, and another was Samson. Einhard, who held the official post of superintendent of public works, was dubbed Beseleel, after the skillful architect who designed the first tabernacle.

Charles's World-Renowned Court

In addition to Einhard, the most intimate of Charles's friends was probably his cousin Adalhard, the abbot of Corbie and a historian who wrote the "Treatise of the

A Rhetorical Dialogue Between Charles and Alcuin

A collection of Alcuin's Dialogues, *dating back to the tenth century, contains several dialogues ostensibly conducted by Alcuin and his most famous student, Charles the Great. Here is an example of one such dialogue, on justice, from Jacob Mombert's* A History of Charles the Great.

"Charles: How is justice subserved by the use of custom?

Alcuin: By pact or agreement; by parity; by judgment; and by law.

Charles: I ask also for more information on these points.

Alcuin: A pact is an agreement reached by mutual consent. Parity is observing equity or impartiality to all men. Judgment is a decision rendered by some great man, or established by the sentence of plurality. Law is right set forth for the whole people, which all are bound to guard and observe. . . .

Charles: . . . Master, you predict some great and truly blessed man.

Alcuin: May God make you great, O lord my king, and truly blessed; may He grant that in the four-span chariot of the virtues, of which we have conversed, you may, unhurt by this wicked world, wing your way to the citadel of heaven.

Charles: God grant that your prediction may come to pass.

Alcuin: I trust that this discussion, which began in the ever-changing whirl of ordinary conversation, may have such a blessed consummation of everlasting stability, that no man may charge us with having only indulged in useless disputings by the way.

Charles: Could any one really interested in the pursuit and investigation of matters so important to society at large, and truly desirous of practicing such excellent virtues, have it in his heart to hazard the daring assertion that our discussion has been in vain? For myself I frankly confess that love of knowledge only has prompted my questions; and I thank you for your kindness in answering them. I highly value the affectionate candor of your replies, and feel convinced that they will be most profitable to all who without prejudice or the blot of envy may sit down and read them."

Order and State of the Palace Throughout the Frankish Realm." Charles consulted Adalhard on important matters and later appointed him as one of his imperial *missi*. Angilbert, who also became an abbot, served as Charles's private counsel and was often called upon to represent the king when the occasion required tact and statesmanship. Besides being a poet of some repute, Angilbert is believed to have been the unofficial husband, or lover, of one of Charles's daughters.

A sure sign of Charles's political power was the number of foreign dignitaries who made arduous journeys to visit him. Caliphs from Cordova, the capital of Is-lamic Spain, popes from Rome, and am-bassadors from Constantinople all came to pay their respects to the king of the Franks. Ireland and southern England were the northern European centers for theology and religious scholarship during this time, and among the scholars who came to Charles's court from that direc-tion was the Irish monk Clement, who as-sisted in establishing schools for the children of the poor.

An interesting story about one mem-ber of Charles's court illustrates the king's great respect for men of learning. Paul the Deacon was a poet and historian who composed a history of the bishops of

Charlemagne's Personal Studies

Charles held great admiration for men of learning, and throughout his adult life he continued his own studies under the instruction of the learned men of his court. In Two Lives of Charlemagne, *Einhard describes these studies.*

"He paid the greatest attention to the liberal arts; and he had great respect for men who taught them, bestowing high honours upon them. When he was learning the rules of grammar he received instruction from Peter the Deacon of Pisa, who by then was an old man, but for all other subjects he was taught by Alcuin, surnamed Albi-nus, another Deacon, a man of the Saxon race who came from Britain and was the most learned man anywhere to be found. Under him the Emperor spent much time and effort in studying rhetoric, dialectic and especially astrol-ogy. He applied himself to mathematics and traced the course of the stars with great attention and care. He also tried to learn to write. With his object in view he used to keep writing-tablets and notebooks under the pillows on his bed, so that he could try his hand at forming letters during his leisure moments; but, although he tried very hard, he had begun too late in life and he made little progress."

Prior to Charles's rule, only the children of nobles received an education. Charles established free schools in villages and monasteries that were open to any boy, regardless of his social status.

Metz, starting with the founder of the Carolingian line, Arnulf. Paul had also spent considerable time at the court of Desiderius, the Lombard king whom Charles had overthrown, and several members of Charles's court were convinced that he was a spy for Desiderius. They shared their suspicion with Charles and recommended the standard punishment for a spy: cutting off his hands and gouging out his eyes. To these charges and recommendations Charles replied, "God forbid that I should thus treat so excellent a poet and a historian."[38]

Students from all social levels and in all parts of the kingdom benefited from Charles's patronage of education. Every monastery had a school, and by royal decree any boy who demonstrated an aptitude for learning—regardless of his family's social status—was educated at no cost to the family. Charles also commanded the clergy to found village schools, and in the duchy of Orleans, Duke Theodulf admonished that "teachers should shine as the brightness of the firmament, and they that turn many to righteousness as the stars forever and ever."[39]

Daily Allowances of the Missi

From Jacob Mombert's A History of Charles the Great *comes this summary of one of Charlemagne's* capitula *concerning the official daily allowances for a single* missus *and his servants. The allowances demonstrate the great value Charles placed on his* missi.

"If the *missus* was a bishop he might feast upon a daily allowance of forty rolls, three fresh hams, three *modii* (a weight measurement) of drink, a young pig, three chickens, fifteen eggs, and four *modii* of horse feed. If he was an abbot, count, or other ministerial officer, he had to content himself with only thirty rolls, two fresh hams, two *modii* of drink, a young pig, three chickens, fifteen eggs, and three *modii* of horse feed; and if he was only a common vassal, his claim must not rise higher than seventeen rolls, a fresh ham, a young pig, one *modius* of drink, two chickens, ten eggs, and two *modii* of horse feed. These were only the major constituents of the daily rations of a *missus*, which consisted altogether of about forty articles, duly described, down to the requisite quantities of pepper, salt, and cinnamon."

Literature, Art, and Architecture

The growth in schools led to greater demands for books, and Charles ordered the monks in his monasteries to copy and collect books. The monks copied religious treatises, classic Latin works, and contemporary histories and chronicles. As a result, the Carolingians created a new form of calligraphy, and they established libraries with hundreds of books at almost every monastery, preserving many Western literary treasures that would otherwise have been permanently lost.

In his letters and capitularies, Charles made clear that monks should study not only the Scriptures but also language and literature in general. In a letter to Baugulf, abbot of Fulda, he admonishes the abbot to emphasize grammar and language studies in his monastery:

We, together with our faithful, have considered it to be useful that the bishoprics and monasteries entrusted by the favor of Christ to our control, in addition, in the culture of letters also ought to be zealous in teaching those who by the gift of God are able to learn, according to the capacity of each individual, so that just as the observance of the rule imparts order and grace to honesty of morals, so also zeal in teaching and learning may do the same for sentences, so that those who desire to please God by living rightly should not neglect to please him also by speaking correctly. . . .

For when in the years just passed letters were often written to us from several monasteries in which it was stated that the brethren who dwelt there offered up in our behalf sacred and pious prayers, we have recognized, in most of these letters, both correct thoughts and uncouth [crude] expressions; because what pious devotion dictated faithfully to the mind, the tongue, uneducated on account of the neglect of study, was not able to express in the letter without error. Whence it happened that we began to fear lest perchance, as the skill in writing was less, so also the wisdom for understanding the Holy Scriptures might be much less than it rightly ought to be.[40]

The monastic libraries founded by Charles became centers for the study of literature, religious art, and architecture. A century later, they became the sites of Europe's first universities. Charles also commissioned architects to erect grand palaces for him at Nimeguen, Ingelheim, and Aachen. He commissioned the greatest architecture, though, for the building of churches, and the greatest of these was the Basilica of St. Mary the Virgin at

Charlemagne oversees the construction of a church. His architectural endeavors included the Basilica of St. Mary the Virgin at Aachen, a bridge across the Rhine River, and a canal from the Rhine to the Danube River.

Aachen. The king's residence at Aachen was named Aix-la-Chapelle, "the place of the chapel." Modeled after St. Peter's in Rome, the basilica itself was said to have been massive yet perfectly symmetrical in style and constructed of exquisitely cut stone. For the interior, Charles imported the choicest marble columns and mosaics from Rome and Ravenna.

Charles's cathedral was severely damaged by an earthquake in the year 829 and rebuilt in a more Gothic style. This later structure was completely destroyed during World War II, but one nineteenth-century observer described the navelike interior:

> It is an octagon in the style of S. Vitale at Ravenna, fifty feet in diameter, surrounded by a sixteen-sided gallery, and terminates in a cupola which in the words of the Saxon poet "climbs to the stars." It is one of the most remarkable monuments of early christian architecture, but unfortunately marred by modern disfigurements.[41]

Breaking New Ground

Charles pushed architectural and engineering knowledge to its extremes. At Mainz he built the first bridge across the Rhine River. The all-wood structure, which required ten years to build, was burned to the ground in 813. At the time of his death one year later, Charles was planning to replace it with an all-stone bridge. Perhaps the boldest construction project of his entire reign, however, was the plan to build a canal from the Rhine River to the Danube that would enable large ships to haul cargo to the eastern extremes of his kingdom. No one had ever attempted to build such a deep canal before, and eventually this project was doomed to failure. To this day, traces of the *Karlsgraben* (Charles's ditch) are visible in southern Germany.

Like his early Spanish campaign, the *Karlsgraben* represents one of Charles's few failures. Yet these are less failures than testimonies to his vision of greatness. Inspired by Alcuin and his circle of close advisers, Charles wanted to renew the borders of the old Roman Empire and replace the old tradition of emperor worship with a new tradition of Christian worship. As the eighth century came to a close, Charles was close to realizing this vision. Except for England, he had reconquered all of Rome's former colonies in Europe, and he had extended the old Roman frontier in Germany all the way to the North Sea. Through his military victories, his government organization, and his patronage of scholars and artists, Charles the Great began a rebirth of civilization.

Chapter

7 The Holy Roman Empire

Strange as it may seem to us today, Charles and his contemporaries did not think of the Roman Empire as a thing of the past. They viewed the Byzantine Empire, with its emperor and capital in Constantinople, as a continuation of the Roman Empire. The loss of Europe to the Franks and other Germanic tribes had diminished the size of the Roman Empire but not what it stood for: civilization, stability, and the tradition of the imperial throne. Although Charles was now king and ruler over the western half of the old Roman Empire, he and his contemporaries still regarded Constantine VI, the boy emperor of Byzantium, as the Roman emperor.

The Byzantine Emperor Is Overthrown

Therefore, in 798 the West was shocked by news that the young emperor had been overthrown by his ambitious mother, Irene, who had ruled as young Constantine's regent for five years after his father died. Charles undoubtedly perceived Irene's revolt as a sign of weakness in the empire and a sign of opportunity for himself.

As long as a legitimate emperor sat on the throne in Constantinople, Charles would not presume to be his rival, or even his equal. Now, however, many Byzantines and western Europeans questioned whether Irene had a legitimate right to reign as empress, and Charles envisioned the possibility that he could be named emperor. The main tie that remained between the West and the Byzantine Empire was Christianity. Just as the Byzantine Empire first emerged as an extension of the Roman Empire, the Eastern Orthodox Church of Byzantium first emerged as an extension of the Church of Rome. And as the protector of the church, Charles believed he had grounds to claim the title of emperor. Here is how G. P. Baker puts it:

Charles was quite capable of a little metaphysical thinking. He had seen his father created (not merely elected) king. Pepin the Short had not been born of royal blood, nor had any of his known ancestors ever possessed the sacred purple. Pepin had been *made* royal, by the election of the Franks and the unction of the pope. There was nothing in the nature of things to prevent the same powers from creating an emperor. And, in any case, no matter what the right or wrong of the electoral power might be, the fact remained that the deposition of

Since the church still held authority in both the eastern and western parts of the old Roman Empire, Charles (right) intended to have Pope Leo III (left) legitimize his claim to become Roman emperor.

Constantine VI created a unique situation. There never before had been any situation in which by any possibility the king of the Franks could become a legitimate emperor. But the possibility had arrived. Charles held the actual powers, the substantial authority. The legal authority might be found.[42]

The Death of Pope Hadrian

Hadrian, the popular and prestigious pope, died in 795, and the bitter disagreement that erupted over his successor, Leo III, gave Charles the opportunity to extend his legal authority. In April 799, a mysterious gang of conspirators attacked and nearly killed Leo. He was taken to a monastery and left to die, but he apparently made a miraculous recovery, escaped from the monastery, and was rescued by the duke of Spoleto, a vassal of Charles.

Even though Charles was the pope's protector, he did not go to Italy immediately to help Leo. Instead, he sent word that Leo should come to him for protection, knowing that the pope had little choice but to comply. Charles gave the excuse that he was engaged in an important council at Paderborn in Saxony and could not travel at the moment; his message effectively reminded Leo who was dependent upon whom.

So Leo came to Paderborn in the fall of 799—the farthest north that any pope had ever traveled. Angilbert described the grand spectacle of this meeting between the two most powerful and revered men in Europe. He also left no doubt about who was in charge of this meeting. It was the pope who knelt before the king and not vice versa:

> At the extremity of the camp the whole [Frankish] army is ordered to halt: the clergy in large numbers, arrayed in sacredotal costume, form into three companies or choirs, ranging themselves under the sacred banner of the cross in an inner circle, round which in ever-widening lines the whole army is disposed like a city wall; in the very center, overtowering all the rest, Charles awaits the pontiff.

> Leo beholds with wondering eyes the magnificent spectacle of that vast multitude, representing so many nationalities collected from all quarters, compacted together, so different in appearance, speech, uniform and arms; it is an overwhelming sight; he looks hither and thither, and beholds Charles coming forth; he lies prostrate in lowly veneration, and rising, gives him a tender, loving welcome in cordial embrace.[43]

When Pope Leo III returned to Rome escorted by an army of Frankish soldiers, his enemies knew that an attack on Leo meant an attack on Charles. At the same time, Leo knew that his dependence on the Frankish king had been revealed to the whole world.

Pope Leo III Appears Before the Court of Charles

In the year 800, Leo's enemies accused him of having used bribery to become pope. This time, any help from Charles was delayed by a personal tragedy. In June 800, Charles's third wife, Liutgarda, died while traveling with the royal court to the city of Tours. She was buried at Tours, some distance from her native country of Alemannia. This city had acquired great

Charles Composes Hadrian's Epitaph

Historians believe that Charles composed the epitaph that was engraved upon Hadrian's tomb. Jacob Mombert included the epitaph in A History of Charles the Great.

"Here sleeps the famous chief, and ornament of
  Rome,
The Father of the Church, Pope Hadrian the blest;
Whom God gave life, the Law his virtue, glory Christ.
An apostolic father to goodness always prompt;
Of grand ancestral line a noble scion he,
More noble than they all, through holiness became.
A faithful pastor with untiring zeal who strove
The temples of his God in beauty to array."

importance as a center of learning, and by this time Charles's adviser Alcuin had become the abbot of Tours. Besides being the site of Liutgarda's funeral, Tours was a central location for Charles to meet with his three sons and his closest advisers, including Alcuin. Charles remained in Tours for three months after Liutgarda's funeral, consulting with Alcuin and meeting with most of his chief vassals. In August, he returned to Aachen, and from there he organized a march to Italy.

Charles and his army arrived in Rome on November 24, 800. He was greeted on the steps of St. Peter's by Pope Leo III, who was surrounded by a host of bishops and priests, "rendering thanks to God and chanting His praises."[44] Charles gave notice that he intended to hold hearings immediately over the accusations against the pope. Although the pope's enemies accused him of numerous crimes against the church, they could show no evidence, and on December 3, 800, Charles ruled in Leo's favor.

Charles Becomes Protector of the Church in Jerusalem

The outcome of the hearings surprised no one. In fact, their singular purpose was for Charles to again emphasize his position not only as protector of the church but also as the highest judge in the land. It was probably more than a mere coincidence, then, that on this very day an im-

---

Queen Liutgarda

Charles's third queen, Liutgarda, was admired by almost all who knew her, both for her physical beauty and for her character. The praises in this letter from the bishop of Orleans, in Mombert's A History of Charles the Great, *are typical.*

"O potent queen, the glory of the great king and of the people, the light and blooming ornament of the Church. May the Father, throned on high, grant long life to you, and thus bless the people and the church of God. You are the light and splendor, the dazzling ornament of all the realm gracing your beauty with the riches of a godly life. Companion of the pious king, you are his well-merited reward, a precious help-mate causing his name to be lauded to the sky. Your outward beauty yields the palm to that within, but I do not venture to say which is first. For beautiful is the burden of your speech; more beautiful your acts, but you yourself are conqueror of both. May God, who gave you the will to do so much good, grant you power to bring it to good effect, and bless you world without end."

portant party of travelers arrived in Rome from the city of Jerusalem.

This party included a priest named Zacharias, an envoy whom Charles had sent to Jerusalem to meet with Haroun al Raschid, the Muslim caliph who then controlled Jerusalem. Zacharias reported that the caliph had offered to recognize Charles as the new protector of the Church of the Holy Sepulcher (the tomb of Jesus) in Jerusalem, an honor previously belonging to the Byzantine emperors. Zacharias gave Charles the keys of the Holy Sepulcher. On the same day that he had tried the pope in his court, Charles had taken yet another symbolic step toward being crowned as emperor.

The First Holy Roman Emperor

The next three weeks were spent celebrating the advent of Christmas and preparing for a glorious Christmas ceremony—the only one that Charles ever spent in Rome. According to Einhard, Pope Leo had especially requested that on Christmas Day Charles wear the traditional Roman dress—a long tunic, a purple robe, and Roman sandals. So attired, and flanked by his sons and his chief vassals, Charles entered the great basilica of St. Peter's on Christmas morning and approached the altar, where the pope, wearing his ceremonial robes, awaited him. Green boughs and purple and gold tapestries were hung from column to column on this high feast day. The altar was glowing with lights, and above it hung a cross composed of 1,370 candles. Beneath the shimmering candles was a screen bearing the painted figures of

Charlemagne's coronation as Holy Roman Emperor by Pope Leo III (pictured) was an elaborate ceremony, complete with traditional Roman clothing, purple and gold tapestries, and hundreds of candles.

angels and saints. The marble floor beneath Charles's feet was marked as the site of St. Peter's tomb.

On cue, Charles alone stepped forward and bowed before the pope. A hush fell over the huge crowd gathered in the nave and around the side sanctuaries of the cathedral. The rustle of the pope's silk vestments broke the silence as he removed something from beneath his robe. As Charles stood, he felt something cold and metallic touch his brow. As one, the thousands of onlookers shouted, "To Charles

The Imperial Fealty Oath

When Charles became emperor, he sent his missi *throughout the realm to secure a new oath of fidelity from every freeman over twelve years of age. As seen in the following* capitula, *translated by Mombert in* A History of Charles the Great, *there were actually two new oaths.*

For those who had sworn an earlier oath:

"I repromise on oath to lord Charles, the most pious emperor, son of King Pepin and Bertrada, that I am faithful as of law a man is bound to be to his master, both as touching his reign and his rights. And this oath, which I have taken, I will, and intend to keep, so far as I know and understand, from this day forth. So help me God, who made heaven and earth, and the patronage of these Saints."

For those who were taking the oath for the first time:

"I promise on oath that from this day forward I am faithful to lord Charles, the most pious emperor, son of King Pepin and Bertrada his queen, with a pure mind, without fraud or malice, of my part to his part, and to the honor of his government, as of law a man is bound to his master. So help me God and the patronage of the Saints, whose relics are in this place, because all the days of my life I will thus attend and of my own free consent, according to the light to me vouchsafed."

Augustus, crowned by God, the great and pacific emperor, life and victory!"[45]

These shouts were not spontaneous. They were part of a carefully orchestrated ritual, and they were followed by the choir and congregation chanting the words of praise and thanksgiving traditionally sung at the coronation of an emperor. Finally, the pope himself knelt, according to the ancient custom, and adored the newly created emperor.

Charles had been named emperor, crowning the sequence of events that he himself had put into play with this well-timed journey to Rome. A great feast and celebration ensued, but if we are to believe Einhard, Charles was not in a mood for celebrating:

It was on this occasion that he received the title of Emperor and Augustus. At first he was far from wanting this. He made it clear that he would not have entered the cathedral that day at all, although it was the greatest of all the festivals of the Church, if he had known in advance what the Pope was planning to do. Once he had accepted the title, he endured with great patience the jealousy of the so-called Roman Emperors, who were most indignant at what had happened.[46]

Could Charles really have been surprised by the coronation? Historians have argued about this since the time it happened. No, many answer, he could not have been surprised. Einhard was just trying to impress his readers with Charles's modesty. After all, he had orchestrated all the events leading up to the coronation. Other historians believe that Charles could have been surprised—not because he did not want the title of emperor, but because he wanted it on his terms. As the last sentence of Einhard's comment suggests, Charles's terms had not been entirely met. Against Charles's wishes, the pope did not simply anoint him as the new emperor; he crowned him. This established the precedent that the pope would always have a say in deciding who became emperor. As a result, the old Roman Empire was restored, at least in theory, as the Holy Roman Empire.

One ruler who seemed pleased by the presence of a Roman emperor in Europe was Haroun al Raschid, the Egyptian caliph. He welcomed this event as a sign of the shrinking of the Byzantine Empire. To show his pleasure, the caliph sent

Haroun al Raschid, the caliph of Egypt, kneels before Charlemagne. The caliph approved of the Frankish king's becoming the Roman emperor, as he thought it would diminish the Byzantine Empire in the east.

Charles a most unique gift. On Charles's return trip from Rome to Aachen, a special delegation from the caliph gave him an elephant, which Charles named Abu-l-Abbas. For several years Abu-l-Abbas, the only elephant in all of Europe, was one of the favorite attractions of the thousands of noblemen, merchants, and other travelers who came to Aachen.

Living Up to the Title of Emperor

Having Charles crowned as emperor changed the daily lives of his subjects very

As Holy Roman Emperor, Charlemagne began to collect and revise the various and sometimes contradictory laws he had written into one compilation called the New Imperial Capitularies.

little. By naming him emperor, the pope had done little more than acknowledge the reality of Charles's rule over almost all the lands of western Europe. Nevertheless, Charles took the change in title extremely seriously, and he immediately set about the task of making his residence in Aachen, and his government, appear more imperial. Rather than traveling from domain to domain as he had in the past, Charles now made Aachen the permanent home of his court, which became an important destination for dignitaries from throughout the civilized world.

Charles's greatest interests during the last stage in his life were affairs of the state, the church, and the intellectual community. The scores of capitularies that he had authored composed a confusing and often contradictory collection of laws. He now devoted a great effort to compiling and refining these into the *New Imperial Capitularies.* According to Einhard:

> He gave much thought to how he could best fill the gaps, reconcile the discrepancies, correct the errors and rewrite the laws which were ill-expressed. None of this was ever finished; he added a few sections, but even these remained incomplete. What he did do was to have collected together and committed to writing the laws of all the nations under his jurisdiction which still remained unrecorded.[47]

Einhard also informs us that Charles consulted Alcuin and others about the most pressing theological issues of his day. One of these was the issue of iconoclasm, or the worship of images and relics, over which the Roman and Eastern Orthodox Churches were seriously split. Charles convened a conference at Tours for leaders of both churches, at which he pronounced his support for the use of icons and relics in Christian worship. With Alcuin, Charles also revised the liturgy of the Frankish church and oversaw a revised Latin translation of the Bible, which became the official translation used by the Roman Church. Finally, Charles commissioned a grammar, or set of rules, for the Frankish language.

The Byzantines Recognize the Holy Roman Empire

One reason that Charles could afford to focus on intellectual matters was that he had three capable sons who now oversaw the empire's military affairs. King Louis of Aquitaine continued to build up the Spanish March; young Charles pursued his father's deportation and resettlement policy in Saxony; and in a direct challenge to Byzantine power in the Mediterranean, King Pepin of Italy placed the independent cities of Venice and Zara under Frankish protection. The Byzantine emperor Nicephorus even sent fleets into the Adriatic to threaten the Franks, but Pepin defeated them.

In the final years of Charles's life, the power of his empire matched that of his two great rivals—the Muslims and the Byzantines. Even though some of Charles's noblemen complained bitterly about his demands for arms and men, few of them ever challenged his authority directly. If Charles's successors had managed to hold onto that authority, the history of Europe might have turned out quite differently.

Charles certainly envisioned something quite different. He had begun to lay the groundwork for his succession when he crowned Louis and Pepin as kings of Aquitaine and Italy, respectively. In the winter of 805, he called his sons to Thionville in the Meuse valley. Together they spent the winter hunting and looking ahead to the future. When the annual assembly of noblemen gathered at Thionville early in 806, Charles clarified his vision for the future of the Holy Roman Empire. After his death, young Charles was to become the new emperor. In addition to the original core of Frankia—including Neustria and Austrasia—young Charles would inherit sovereignty over Saxony, Thuringia, Alemannia, and Burgundy. Pepin, whose kingdom was to include Italy and Bavaria, and Louis, who was to reign over Aquitaine, Provence, and the March of Spain, would both be vassals to their older brother.

If these divisions had remained in place, France and Germany as we know them would not exist. In their place, one great nation, stretching from the Eider River in eastern Germany to the Loire River in central France and from the Baltic Sea to the Alps, would dominate western Europe.

A New Threat Appears in the North

Even before Charles's death, cracks began to develop in his plan, resulting from both internal and external threats. In the north, a new military power, the Danes, was on the rise. As horsemanship had given the Franks a decided advantage over their enemies, so the Danes introduced a new military force to northern Europe: naval

The Proposed Division of Charles's Empire

Charles
Pepin
Louis

} TRIBUTARY LANDS

NORTH SEA

BALTIC SEA

NORTH ATLANTIC OCEAN

Frisia
Saxony
Slavs
Verden
Paderborn
Thuringia
AACHEN
Austrasia
Czechs
Brittany
France
Neustria
Alemannia
Fontenoy
Burgundy
Bavaria
Aquitaine
Lombardia
Gascony
Provence
Septimania
Papal States
Spanish March
Barcelona
Corsica
Rome
Duchy of Benevento
Cordova
Sardinia
Balearic Islands
Byzantine Empire
Sicily

MEDITERRANEAN SEA

power. In 808 Danish armies under their king, Guthfrith, landed on the shores of Wihmodia, north of the Elbe River. In response, Charles called an assembly and sent young Charles to lead an army to Saxony, but before the Frankish army could assemble, the Danes had pushed the Saxons all the way back to the Elbe River.

Young Charles forced the Danes to retreat, but his father, realizing that the Danish threat was not going to disappear,

knew that the Franks needed a more permanent presence on the Elbe. Therefore, he commissioned the building of a city called Esselfeld, to be garrisoned by Frankish soldiers, and he offered land to Frankish vassals willing to relocate in this northern fortress. Esselfeld was the origin of the great modern German port of Hamburg. Following the death of Guthfrith, a new Danish king, Heming, sent emissaries to Aachen to offer peace to

Charles. Charles accepted Heming's entreaties, but he still foresaw the time when the Danes, with their powerful navies, would demand a share of his empire.

One Surviving Heir

In the meantime, Charles's plans for the division of the empire after his death received a serious setback when two of his three heirs died within eighteen months of each other. On July 8, 810, his son Pepin, the king of Italy, died. This in itself did not upset Charles's succession plans because Pepin's young son Bernard was named as the new Italian king. Just a little over a year later, however, on December 4, 811, young Charles died at the age of thirty-nine. Einhard tells us that Charles took the losses of his children extremely hard:

> He bore the death of his two sons and his daughter [Rotrude, who died in 810 also] with less fortitude than one would have expected, considering the strength of his character; for his emotions as a father, which were very deeply rooted, made him burst into tears.[48]

The death of young Charles, his oldest son and heir to the imperial throne, must have been especially difficult for Charles to accept. He had placed his hopes for the empire in this son. To make matters worse, young Charles died without an heir. Thus the emperor's personal grief was compounded by new complications for the future of the empire. Charles had envisioned the three royal houses of his sons complementing one another and sustaining his empire just as they had while he was alive. That all changed with the death of young Charles.

Now Louis, the only one of Charles's three legitimate sons still living, was in line to inherit the lands intended for young

---

Charlemagne Foresees Trouble

According to the Monk of St. Gall, Charles foresaw the danger that the Danes posed and he wept for the future of his empire.

"Charles, who was a God-fearing, just and devout ruler, rose from the table and stood at a window facing east. For a long time the precious tears poured down his face. No one dared to ask him why. In the end he explained his behavior to his warlike leaders. 'My faithful servants,' said he, 'do you know why I wept so bitterly? I am not afraid that these ruffians will be able to do me any harm; but I am sick at heart to think that even in my lifetime they have dared to attack this coast, and I am horror-stricken when I foresee what evil they will do to my descendants and their subjects.'"

Charles. Charles the Great was reluctant to give Louis so much land and power, along with the title of emperor, but he saw no other alternative. Nearly two years went by before Charles made the decision official. In September 813 the emperor called his last general assembly and crowned Louis as his sole successor.

Charles's closest adviser, Alcuin, was pleased by this turn of events. Alcuin, who had been Louis's teacher, had always favored Louis over his brothers. Louis was a bright scholar, a lover of literature and the arts, and also a modest, deeply religious young man. He was the kind of person who, Alcuin believed, would make an ideal emperor. That may be why, according to Alcuin's anonymous biographer, the abbot predicted Louis's accession and rejoiced in it:

> The king, holding Alcuin by the hand, asked him in a low voice: "Tell me, master mine, which of these my three sons will in your opinion succeed me in the honors which God on me unworthy has bestowed?" Alcuin directed his eye on Louis and said, "The humble Louis will be your excellent successor."

> Only the king heard what he said. They entered the Church of St. Stephen, and Alcuin noticing the attitude of the royal brothers, Charles and Pepin with their heads proudly erect,

Charles (left) pondered for months whether to leave his empire to his last surviving son, Louis. Finally, in 813, he made his decision and young Louis was crowned as his successor (right).

Charles's son Louis (pictured) was favored by Alcuin as successor to his father's empire. Louis had a gift for scholastics, a devotion to Christianity, and a humble disposition.

but Louis meekly bowing his, said to those around him: "Do you see Louis more humble than his brothers? Verily you will behold him as the most illustrious successor of his father."[49]

The Death of Charles the Great

At about this time, Charles also began to lose his vigorous good health. A year earlier, on a trip to Verden, Charles had taken a hard fall from his horse, and from that time on, according to Einhard, he began to suffer from fevers. Still, he insisted on staying active, and in May 813 he badly injured his foot while on a hunting expe-

dition in the Ardennes. The injury did not heal properly, leaving Charles with a pronounced limp for the rest of his days.

In January 814 Charles was confined to bed with a fever worse than he had experienced previously. Finally the great king, soldier, statesman, and scholar found something that he did not do well. He was a most impatient and miserable patient. Unwilling to listen to his own doctors, he decided that the best cure for his illness was fasting, and so he proceeded to fast with great severity and willpower. Unfortunately, the treatment only increased his fever and made him weaker. On the morning of January 28, at the age of seventy-two, he received his last communion at his palace in Aachen and died. Charles was buried at the Basilica of St. Mary the Virgin in Aachen, the church that he had built. The tomb was marked with a life-size statue of Charles in his imperial robes, and on the tomb was engraved this epitaph:

> Within this tomb lies the body of Charles the Great and the Orthodox Emperor, who nobly extended the Frankish realm and prosperously reigned for forty-seven years. He departed this life, over seventy years of age, in the eight hundred and fourteenth year of Our Lord, in the seventh indiction, on the fifth day before the kalends of February.[50]

The Reign of Louis the Pious

Louis became the second and last ruler of the united Frankish empire. Louis was a remarkable man in his own right, and in many ways he was far different from his

A view of Charlemagne's coffin. The emperor's death in 814 left his son Louis emperor; Louis would become the last ruler of the united Frankish kingdom his father built.

father. Although he had represented himself well in the Spanish campaigns, he probably owed this success to the military genius and leadership of his vassal Count William of Toulouse, a close friend of Charles the Great.

Unlike his father and his two brothers, Louis was not particularly athletic. He did, however, inherit his father's love of learning, and he was a disciple of Alcuin, the founder of Charles's palace school. In fact, Louis was such a strong and devoted patron of the church and the arts that he was called Louis the Pious. Under his enthusiastic leadership, the churches, monasteries, schools, and libraries of the empire flourished; historians call his reign the high point of the Carolingian renaissance.

The differences between Louis and his father are most evident in the way he managed his household and his empire. In personal affairs, Louis was far more like his monastic teachers than like his Frankish father. He took the church's teachings and admonitions regarding monogamy more seriously than Charles had. He not only practiced it, he condemned any violation of it as sinful. His father, for example, had encouraged all Louis's sisters to keep unofficial mates, because he did not trust any of their official suitors. When Louis became master of the palace, he banished these unofficial husbands from the palace.

Louis also took the idea of a Holy Roman Emperor seriously. Perhaps even more than his father, he envisioned the greatness of the state above the greatness of its king or emperor. His revised capitularies of 819 and 820 demonstrate a clarity and order that were missing from Charles's capitularies. The principle behind these ordinances was Louis's vision of the permanence of the state and of the state's superiority over the power of any individual.

Louis's capitularies were meant as a model to be followed at every level of government, and when a count or duke died, his oldest son would inherit not only a title and a fief but also a set of laws to rule by.

Louis also attempted to reform the general assemblies, which usually gave

Although Louis was adept at clarifying and organizing the capitularies his father had written, he did not command the respect of his vassals that Charlemagne had, nor did he actively engage in military conquests to expand the empire.

their rubber stamp approval to Charles's decrees and served as a preamble to his annual military campaigns. Louis gave the assemblies their own status separate from any military purpose. They were to be administrative sessions in which the emperor could hear from his noblemen, take their advice, and also exercise more effective influence on these local rulers. Louis also encouraged greater influence by the church in these assemblies.

The Breakup of the Holy Roman Empire

Despite Louis's vision and intellectual leadership, however, most historians look upon his reign as the beginning of the empire's decline. They often blame the decline on Louis's weakness as a leader. While that view may be unfair or oversimplified, it holds some truth. Under Charles the Great, general assemblies were always linked to some military campaign. All the freemen in the land were required to attend these assemblies and join the military campaigns or else contribute supplies and weapons. Under Louis the Pious, general assemblies were often called without any military purpose, and when his vassals began ignoring the general assemblies, Louis did not discipline them.

Historians are fond of saying that Louis did not command the same loyalty from his vassals that Charles had. It may be closer to the truth to say that Louis did not engage in continual campaigns of conquest, as his father had. Although Charles's vassals complained bitterly about fulfilling their military obligation, these campaigns had been extraordinarily beneficial to the Frankish kingdom and empire. Not only did they add greatly to the size and prestige of the kingdom, they also kept the Frankish noblemen from fighting among themselves for personal gain.

It may be that Louis the Pious was just too good a person to be a good emperor. His greatest weakness was probably his willingness to trust others. He seemed unwilling to recognize that those he entrusted with power were often motivated by greed and jealousy. After the death of Charles the Great, many Frankish noblemen began to use their military might for their own gain rather than to help the empire.

Greed and jealousy also seemed to motivate Louis's four sons. Rather than mutually supporting one another, after their father's death in 840, the three surviving brothers fought over territory and over rights of vassalage. Finally, in 841 they met in a terrible battle, the Battle of Fontenoy. This battle renewed many ancient feuds, including that between the houses of Neustria and Austrasia. When Louis's son Lothair was defeated at the Battle of Fontenoy, the great Austrasian house founded by Charlemagne's great-great-grandfather, St. Arnulf, was forever eliminated from royalty and power.

The Treaty of Verdun

The outcome of the Battle of Fontenoy was the Treaty of Verdun, signed by Louis's three surviving sons in 843. They divided Charlemagne's empire into three kingdoms. Although their borders would be amended and refined over the next eleven and a half centuries, these three kingdoms eventually became the nations of France, Germany, and Italy. The name Holy Roman Empire remained, but it applied only to a network of German dukes and counts who were allied with the Roman Church and vassals of an emperor whom they elected from among themselves.

Charlemagne's Legacy

Although Charlemagne's united empire lasted only twenty-nine years after his death, the effects of his empire are still felt today. Though the nations of Italy, France, and Germany gradually developed their own national identities, Charles had lifted them out of the chaos created by the Germanic invasions and into the order of self-disciplined political states.

He also managed to place an extraordinary amount of European soil under the rule of his handpicked vassals. The descendants of these men formed the highest levels of Europe's noble class for the next eleven centuries. Until the modern age, Europeans identified themselves far more closely with their class than with their nation. Long after the boundaries drawn up by the Treaty of Verdun had been erased and redrawn dozens of times, the rulers of the resulting nations, duchies, marches, and counties came mostly from the descendants of Charles's vassals. They often married among themselves, so that kings, dukes, and other great barons of all the European nations were related to one another. Whether related or not, a Bavarian duke had far more in common with a French count than with a peasant or a craftsman from his own village.

Regardless of their geographical locations, these noblemen communicated with

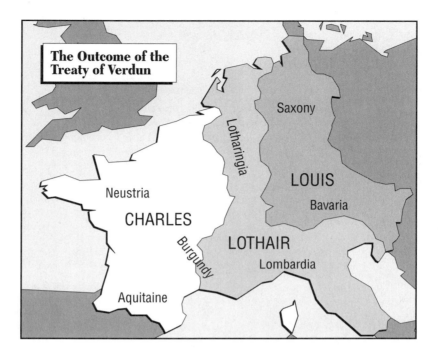

The Outcome of the Treaty of Verdun

one another in the same language—Latin, they swore the same feudal oaths, and they observed the same social and religious customs. Most of their ancestors were Franks, and they even shared the Frankish zeal for independence. Although this zeal broke the Frankish empire into pieces, it united the noble class of Europe under the code of feudalism. Despite developing as distinct nations with distinct languages, customs, and laws, the unity of the noble classes dating back to the time of Charlemagne caused the nations of Europe to develop along common paths. They may have spoken different languages and worn different costumes, but they observed common principles of government, religion, and commerce. Their rulers lived, married, traded, and warred among themselves.

Since 841, the Battle of Fontenoy has been replayed hundreds of times among the noble houses on hundreds of battlefields throughout Europe. The continent has been splintered into more than a dozen different nations, and yet the foundation of the military, political, religious, and economic histories of all the nations of Western Europe can be traced back to the short-lived but glorious empire of Charles the Great.

Notes

Chapter 1: The Rise of the Franks

1. Quoted in Brian Pullan, ed., *Sources for the History of Medieval Europe*. Oxford: Basil Blackwell, 1966.

2. *Annals of Metz*, quoted in Pierre Riché, *The Carolingians: A Family Who Forged Europe*. Translated by Michael Idomir Allen. Philadelphia: University of Pennsylvania Press, 1993.

3. *Annals of Metz*, quoted in Pierre Riché, *The Carolingians*.

Chapter 2: Founders of the Carolingian Dynasty

4. Pope Gregory III, quoted in Pierre Riché, *The Carolingians*.

5. *Royal Frankish Annals*, quoted in Pullan, *Sources for the History of Medieval Europe*.

6. *Annals of Metz*, quoted in Pierre Riché, *The Carolingians*.

7. *Clausula de Unctione Pippini*, quoted in Pullan, *Sources for the History of Medieval Europe*.

8. *Clausula de Unctione Pippini*, quoted in Pullan, *Sources for the History of Medieval Europe*.

9. *Clausula de Unctione Pippini*, quoted in Pullan, *Sources for the History of Medieval Europe*.

10. *Royal Frankish Annals*, quoted in Pullan, *Sources for the History of Medieval Europe*.

11. *Royal Frankish Annals*, quoted in Pullan, *Sources for the History of Medieval Europe*.

Chapter 3: Charlemagne's Kingdom

12. Einhard, *Two Lives of Charlemagne*. Translated by Lewis Thorpe. Baltimore: Penguin Books, 1969.

13. Einhard, *Two Lives of Charlemagne*.

14. Einhard, *Two Lives of Charlemagne*.

15. Einhard, *Two Lives of Charlemagne*.

16. Einhard, *Two Lives of Charlemagne*.

17. Einhard, *Two Lives of Charlemagne*.

18. Einhard, *Two Lives of Charlemagne*.

19. Einhard, *Two Lives of Charlemagne*.

20. Einhard, *Two Lives of Charlemagne*.

21. Einhard, *Two Lives of Charlemagne*.

22. Einhard, *Two Lives of Charlemagne*.

23. Einhard, *Two Lives of Charlemagne*.

Chapter 4: Expanding the Frankish Kingdom

24. Quoted in Brian Tierney, ed., *The Middle Ages: Sources of Medieval History*, 4th ed., vol. 1. Translated by D. C. Munro. New York: Alfred Knopf, 1983.

25. *Capitularia Regum Francorum*, quoted in Jacob Isidor Mombert, *A History of Charles the Great*. Translated by Boredius. New York: D. Appleton and Company, 1888.

26. Mombert, *A History of Charles the Great*.

27. Einhard, *Two Lives of Charlemagne*.

28. Einhard, *Two Lives of Charlemagne*.

29. Einhard, *Two Lives of Charlemagne*.

30. George Philip Baker, *Charlemagne and the United States of Europe*. New York: Dodd, Mead and Company, 1932.

Chapter 5: The Founding of the German Nation

31. Einhard, *Two Lives of Charlemagne.*
32. Einhard, *Two Lives of Charlemagne.*
33. Einhard, *Two Lives of Charlemagne.*
34. Quoted in Tierney, *The Middle Ages.*
35. *Annals of Nazariani,* quoted in Mombert, *A History of Charles the Great.*

Chapter 6: A Prosperous Kingdom

36. Einhard, *Two Lives of Charlemagne.*
37. Einhard, *Two Lives of Charlemagne.*
38. Quoted in Monk of St. Gall, *Charles the Great.* Translated by Lewis Thorpe. Baltimore: Penguin Books, 1969.
39. Theodulf, *Carmina,* quoted in Mombert, *A History of Charles the Great.*
40. Quoted in Tierney, *The Middle Ages.*
41. Quoted in Mombert, *A History of Charles the Great.*

Chapter 7: The Holy Roman Empire

42. Baker, *Charlemagne and the United States of Europe.*
43. Quoted in Mombert, *A History of Charles the Great.*
44. Einhard, *Two Lives of Charlemagne.*
45. *Liber Pontificalis,* quoted in Pullan, *Sources for the History of Medieval Europe.*
46. Einhard, *Two Lives of Charlemagne.*
47. Einhard, *Two Lives of Charlemagne.*
48. Einhard, *Two Lives of Charlemagne.*
49. Quoted in Baker, *Charlemagne and the United States of Europe.*
50. *Royal Frankish Annals,* quoted in Pullan, *Sources for the History of Medieval Europe.*

Glossary

abbey: Land or village owned or once owned by the Roman Catholic Church, usually surrounding a monastery.

abbot: The church official who is lord of the abbey.

annals: Written historical records organized year by year. In the Middle Ages, most monasteries kept them.

anoint: To place oil on a person's head as a sacred consecration.

aristocracy: The ruling class; nobility.

autonomy: Self-government.

bishop: The highest rank of priesthood; the priest generally in charge of all church matters within his diocese, or bishopric.

bishopric: The region or district controlled by a single bishop.

Byzantine Empire: The eastern part of the later Roman Empire, founded by Constantine in A.D. 330 and continuing until 1453; its capital was Constantinople.

caliph: The religious head of a Muslim state.

capitula: Ordinances; laws.

capitulary: A collection of *capitula.*

Carolingian: Of or related to the dynasty of Frankish kings founded by Charles Martel in approximately 737.

centurion: An officer commanding one hundred soldiers. Clovis and his descendants adopted this title from the Romans and applied it to members of the Frankish nobility.

cleric: A member of the clergy.

count: The noble title given to the lord of a county.

deacon: A young man training for the priesthood.

duke: The noble title given to the lord of a duchy.

dynasty: A succession of rulers from the same family line.

fealty: A vassal's obligation to be loyal; homage.

feudalism: The economic system of private government and military organization based on oaths between lords and vassals. In return for a promise of loyalty and military service, the lord granted his vassal a fief.

feudal oath: The vow sworn by both lord and vassal to uphold the conditions of their agreement. The vassal swore his loyalty and promised military service, while the lord promised to honor and protect the vassal's fief.

fief: The fee that a lord granted to his vassal, usually in the form of land.

freeman: Anyone who was not a serf or a slave.

Gaul: The name given by the Romans to the area of Europe that is now called France.

Great Migration: The movement of Germanic tribes from eastern Europe into western Europe and the British Isles, predominantly in the fourth and fifth centuries.

hierarchy: A system with higher and lower ranks of power.

homage: A vassal's loyalty to his lord.

idol: An image used as an object of worship.

infidel: Term used by Christians of the Middle Ages to mean a non-Christian, especially a Muslim.

investiture: The act of conferring a title or office on another.

Levant: The countries bordering on the eastern Mediterranean.

manse: A medieval land measurement, roughly enough land to support a single man.

march: A frontier territory gained by military conquest, such as the Spanish March or the March of Brittany.

mayor of the palace: The highest ranking member of a Merovingian king's court.

Merovingian: Of or related to the dynasty of Frankish kings who were descendants of the warrior Meroveus and who ruled over Gaul from about 500 until 751.

monastery: A place where monks live and work.

monk: A man who belongs to a religious order whose members live in a monastery.

nativity: Birth, most often used in referring to the birth of Jesus.

pagan: One who worships non-Christian gods.

patronage: Support, usually financial.

regent: An acting ruler.

Saracen: An Arab.

scurrilous: Being vulgar or evil.

secularize: To draw away from religious interest toward a worldly interest.

surety: A guarantee or oath; a promise.

vassal: A nobleman who swore homage to another nobleman.

vicar: A deputy or representative.

villa: A country residence.

viscount: A deputy count.

For Further Reading

Isaac Asimov, *The Dark Ages*. Boston: Houghton Mifflin, 1968. Though its illustrations and maps are weak, this is still an informative and well-written history of Europe from the time of the fall of Rome to the end of the Carolingian period. It includes an excellent time line as well as genealogical tables of the Merovingian and Carolingian kings.

Susan Banfield, *Charlemagne*. New York: Chelsea House, 1986. A short, illustrated biography of the life of Charlemagne.

Timothy Levi Biel, *The Age of Feudalism*. San Diego: Lucent Books, 1994. A thorough history and explanation of the political and economic system that dominated Europe and shaped European nobility beginning roughly at the time of Charlemagne. The book includes a large number of historical photographs and maps, a helpful time line, and numerous excerpts from primary sources.

Morris Bishop, *The Horizon Book of the Middle Ages*. New York: American Heritage, 1968. A thorough overview of the cultural, political, and intellectual history of the Middle Ages. Filled with photographs and reprints of medieval artifacts.

Polly Schoyer Brooks and Nancy Zinsses Walworth, *The World of Walls: The Middle Ages in Western Europe*. Philadelphia: J. P. Lippincott, 1966. A richly illustrated overview of the history of the Middle Ages for the young adult reader. Approximately one-third of this book is devoted to the early Middle Ages.

James A. Corrick, *The Early Middle Ages*. San Diego: Lucent Books, 1995. Covers the period of Charlemagne's reign.

David Edge and John Miles Paddock, *Arms and Armor of the Medieval Knight*. New York: Crescent Books, 1988. A history of knights from their barbarian and Roman beginnings through the sixteenth century. With an abundance of photographs of authentic armor and weapons, this book presents an interesting perspective on medieval times.

Abigail Frost, *The Age of Chivalry*. New York: Marshall Cavendish, 1990. A colorfully illustrated overview for young readers of the manners, customs, and values of medieval nobility, many of which are traced back to the time of Charlemagne.

Tony Gregory, *The Dark Ages*. New York: Facts On File, 1993. An excellent, illustrated history of Europe from the fall of Rome through the time of Charlemagne.

Jennifer Westwood, *Stories of Charlemagne*. New York: S. G. Phillips, 1976. A collection of biographical stories and legends about Charlemagne. Taken from original sources such as Einhard and the Monk of St. Gall, these stories have been adapted for the young reader.

Martin Windrow, *The Medieval Knight*. New York: Franklin Watts, 1985. An illustrated portrayal of the training, weapons, and lifestyle of a typical medieval knight, with glossary and time line.

Works Consulted

George Philip Baker, *Charlemagne and the United States of Europe.* New York: Dodd, Mead, and Company, 1932. One of the most quotable studies of Charlemagne in the English language. The strength of Baker's work is its lucid clarification of the importance of Charlemagne's contribution to the culture of Europe.

Jacques Boussard, *The Civilization of Charlemagne.* New York: McGraw Hill, 1968. Rather than a chronological study, this is an analysis of social institutions in Frankish civilization, including the nobility, the church, the government, education, and economic institutions. A series of maps illustrates the evolution of the Frankish empire from approximately 750 to 880.

Clausula de Unctione Pippini, quoted in Brian Pullan, ed., *Sources for the History of Medieval Europe.* Translated by B. Krusch. Oxford: Basil Blackwell, 1966.

Einhard, *Two Lives of Charlemagne.* Translated by Lewis Thorpe. Baltimore: Penguin Books, 1969.

Henry William Carless Davis, *Charlemagne: The Hero of Two Nations.* New York: G. P. Putnam's Sons, 1899. Davis's timeless biography of Charlemagne remains one of the most interesting works of its kind. Engagingly written, it contains a treasury of plates that illustrate what life in the court of Charlemagne must have been like. It also includes genealogical tables, maps, and a time line of important dates.

Francois Louis Ganshof, *The Carolingians and the Frankish Monarchy: Studies in Carolingian History.* Ithaca, NY: Cornell University Press, 1971. A helpful interpretation of the cultural, philosophical, and political impact of the Carolingian monarchy on European history.

Gregory of Tours, *History of the Franks.* Oxford: The Clarendon Press, 1927. The oldest known complete history of the Franks written by a member of the Frankish court.

Edward James, *The Origins of France, from Clovis to the Capetians.* New York: St. Martin's Press, 1982. An extremely helpful guide to the foundation of Frankia. This book has excellent photographs, genealogical tables, maps, and bibliographies.

Liber Pontificalis, quoted in Brian Pullan, ed., *Sources for the History of Medieval Europe.* Translated by L. Duchesne.

Rosemond McKitterick, ed., *Carolingian Culture: Emulation and Innovation.* Cambridge: Cambridge University Press, 1994. A collection of essays by modern scholars on the emergence of art, music, literature, and philosophy during the Carolingian period. Superior documentation and fascinating illustrations, including music scores composed during this period.

Jacob Isidor Mombert, *A History of Charles the Great.* New York: D. Appleton and Company, 1888. Though some of the grandeur and heroism in this portrayal of Charlemagne has been challenged by modern scholars, Mombert's study is a classic model of thoroughness. It is probably the single most complete collection of primary quotations from Charlemagne and his contemporaries.

Monk of St. Gall, *Charles the Great.* Translated by Lewis Thorpe. Baltimore: Penguin Books, 1969.

Frederick Ogg, ed., *A Source Book of Medieval History.* New York: American Book Company, 1907.

Pseudo Fredegar, *The Chronicle of Fredegar.* Translated by J. M. Wallace-Hadrill. London: Nelson, 1960.

Brian Pullan, ed., *Sources for the History of Medieval Europe.* Oxford: Basil Blackwell, 1966.

Pierre Riché, *The Carolingians: A Family Who Forged Europe.* Translated by Michael Idomir Allen. Philadelphia: University of Pennsylvania Press, 1993. A recent analysis of the important influence of the Carolingians, which makes excellent use of previous scholarship. Filled with useful information and quotations from primary and secondary sources such as the *Annals of Metz,* the documentation for which often seems incomplete.

Royal Frankish Annals, quoted in Brian Pullan, ed., *Sources for the History of Medieval Europe.* Translated by G. H. Pertz and F. Kurtze.

Richard Sullivan, *The Coronation of Charlemagne: What Did It Signify?* Boston: Heath, 1959. A collection of both primary accounts and modern scholarly interpretations of Charlemagne's transition from king to emperor.

Richard Winston, *Charlemagne: From the Hammer to the Cross.* Indianapolis: Bobbs-Merrill, 1954. Authoritative, carefully documented biography. Though it contains no maps or illustrations, the text makes lively reading.

Index

Credits

About the Author

Timothy Levi Biel was born and raised in eastern Montana. A graduate of Rocky Mountain College, he received a Ph.D. in literary studies from Washington State University. He taught college English for several years and is currently a research manager for a software development company.

He is the author of numerous nonfiction books, many of which are part of the highly acclaimed Zoobooks series for young readers, in addition to *Pompeii: World Disasters, The Age of Feudalism, The Crusades,* and several other books for Lucent Books.